G000254344

From Santa María with I

From Santa María
with Love

Margaret Hebblethwaite

DARTON·LONGMAN + TODD

First published in 2011 by
Darton, Longman and Todd Ltd
1 Spencer Court
140 – 142 Wandworth High Street
London SW18 4JJ

© 2011 Margaret Hebblethwaite

The right of Margaret Hebblethwaite to be identified as the Author of this work has
been asserted in accordance with the Copyright, Designs and Patents Act 1998.

ISBN: 978-0-232-52885-5

A catalogue record for this book is available from the British Library.
Printed and bound in Great Britain by Page Bros, Norwich, Norfolk.

Contents

Contents

Contents

Foreword

I am sitting in my garden in Santa María de Fe, Misiones, Paraguay, watching an emerald hummingbird dart from flower to flower. The *picaflor*, or *mainumbý* as it is known in the local language of Guaraní, is just one of the delights of this little-known country in which I have the privilege of living. Its rapid movement – never settling to eat, but sampling while hovering in mid-flight – reminds me of the pressure that has accompanied all my writing here. I have snatched a few hours to write a column, and then rushed off and found no more time to compose until the monthly deadline loomed up again.

When I gave up my job at *The Tablet* to emigrate to Paraguay, I thought I would have the time to write a lot of books, having written a number of books before I went to work at *The Tablet* and even while I was still working there. But in fact the needs of the people, and my desire to respond in a small way to them, has eaten up my time and meant that ten years passed before I published a single book – and then it was one that was quite different to anything I had ever written before. The *Bradt Guide to Paraguay* was written out of the conviction that an English-language guide to the country was an urgent necessity.

From Santa María with Love is the second book I have published while living in Paraguay, but I sincerely hope it will not be my last. It is not a new creation, but rather a compilation of edited columns from the international Catholic weekly *The Tablet*, which I wrote monthly from September 2000 (when I came to live in Paraguay) until the series came to an end in December 2010. With one exception, everything in this book has been published in some form before in *The Tablet*, but this attractive edition prepared by Darton, Longman and Todd brings them together in a way that provides a sweeping overview of the joys and struggles of a poor Latin American country over the course of a decade.

The one piece that has not been published before is 'The pig' (p.54), which John Wilkins, *The Tablet*'s editor at the time, refused to print. I thought it rather a good piece and kept sending him emails headed 'This little piggy' and 'Honk, honk' to ask when it was going to appear. Eventually, after a delay of two and a half months, he replied as follows: 'MARGARET, the pig! How ON EARTH did you think I could publish that in *The Tablet*? I read it with appalled fascination. When it appears in one of your books, no one will forget it. But Deborah Jones, who has just written a Viewpoint for *The Tablet* about how pigs should be provided with manipulable toys, would have a heart attack, and she would not be alone.' Now at last we have the opportunity to test out that prediction.

My monthly column was originally commissioned by John Wilkins in 2000, and continued when Catherine Pepinster became editor in 2004. It was called *From the South*, until January 2005, when it became just *Margaret Hebblethwaite*, and acquired a rather unflattering photo of me, sporting the plait that I used to have as a gesture of solidarity with indigenous hairstyles. In April 2006 the design of the column changed a little again, and the word count went down from 850 to 800 words, but most of the pieces in this book are a little longer than that, as I have been able to re-incorporate material that I had to cut before, to make my copy fit into the box assigned to it. I would regularly write on the long side, and then pare down.

I have kept the chronological order of publication, with few exceptions. Some editing changes have been made for this edition, and where the piece contained information now out of date, I have added a comment in italics at the end. But I have not attempted to update the piece to make it seem written in 2011: I prefer to present a history of the decade – Santa María's history, Paraguay's history, and my history.

Looking back over those ten years, I can see a number of important changes here in Santa María. Today, Paraguay is slowly developing – perhaps behind nearly every other South American country, but still making a little progress year by year. In the early years of this millennium, however, the poverty was increasing and we felt we were going backwards. The dollar multiplied its value against the guaraní by two and a half times between 2000 and 2003, so it was inevitable that people became poorer. Then Argentina went through its catastrophic crisis, when it had committed itself to parity between the peso and the dollar but could not sustain its promise, and its economy almost collapsed. Since almost every Paraguayan family has members living in Argentina, sending money home, this crisis hit us hard, and many Paraguayans returned penniless to the country whose poverty they had once fled. A friend said to me then about the poverty: 'It has always been bad, but I have never known it as bad as this.'

When I arrived here in 2000, I was almost the only person in Santa María with a mobile phone, and one of only three people with a computer. I struggled for months to get any sort of an internet connection, and eventually found a way of getting emails out, stumblingly, unreliably and occasionally, via my neighbour's phone line. Today, around fifty homes in Santa María have a computer and many of them have an internet connection too. Every family now has a mobile phone number that they can use – if not of someone in the household, then of a relative or neighbour; they will not use it for outgoing calls, but it can be used for incoming calls or for texting urgent messages.

Before I came to Paraguay and was wondering which country to live in, a journalist friend said, 'You want to go to a country with good communications.' I did not quite know what good communications meant, having never experienced bad ones, but I was now beginning to find out.

When I first arrived, I could not buy a newspaper in Santa María. Today I have one delivered to my door every day. When I first arrived, almost everyone travelled on foot or by bus. Today, many people travel by motor bike. When I first arrived, I had to go a four-hour journey to Asunción every month to pay my mobile phone bill and to draw out money on my credit card. Today, our neighbouring town of San Ignacio has five banks and three cash machines.

But we are still underdeveloped. Massive and chronic unemployment is still the scourge that separates mothers from children and husbands from wives, as people have to go far away to look for work, often abroad. Nearly everyone has electricity, but nearly everyone still struggles to pay their monthly bill, even though it may be for only a couple of pounds. Most people still live hand to mouth, buying their groceries from their corner shop on credit, and spending any earnings just as soon as they get them, as they pay off the instalments on their debts.

When it rains, children still do not go to school and adults do not go to work, because the roads are impassable. When it rains, the lights still go out at times and the toilet does not flush (because the water pumps depend on electricity) and you still have to unplug your computer to avoid it getting destroyed by lightning. And it rains a lot, which is a blessing in a hot country.

One thing that has not changed is the love that the people show. When I first came I was nervous about whether or not I would be accepted. I need not have worried. Paraguayans have big hearts and open arms, and their greeting, even to strangers, is a kiss on both cheeks. They may be shy, and they may be poor, but they know how to make you welcome. So this book comes to you infused not with my love, but with the love of the people of Santa María.

1

On the brink

Why Paraguay? Many people have asked me this since I announced my intention to go there for at least a year. How can one explain matters of the heart? I felt foolish when I told them, 'Because there the earth is red.'

'It stains', complained a Spanish priest working in the *campo*, unromantically. True. When I came back from my visit last year my white trainers had taken on an unremovable red hue. Now, sitting in the airport in August 2000, tapping on my palm top, waiting for the plane to take me off on this adventure of a lifetime, I look down at those same trainers. Yes, you cannot get rid of it: around the crack between sole and upper is the reddish brown mark of Paraguayan earth, that has lingered there for 16 months, carrying me back to its native land.

This year will not be an easy one. Unlike many third-world countries where rich and poor live side by side, Paraguay's capital has not even the facade of a bright, shiny city. The austerity I am facing on all sides does not decrease my desire for good food and drink, but rather increases it. I am hoping not to have to emulate the Sisters who live in the *campo* I am heading towards, in sleeping three to a room.

But I want to go. I have wanted to go – in broad terms, to go somewhere in Latin America – since my husband Peter died in 1994 and I decided to do something positive with this new stage in my life. I have wanted to go – specifically, to Santa María de Fe in Misiones – since 1996, when I spent an hour in the village, fell in love with it, and immediately said shyly to my guide, 'Maybe one day I will come back and live here.' Now, in 2000, because my youngest child has reached 18, I am free to fulfil the longheld dream. My four heavy boxes of indispensable books are already awaiting me in Asunción.

My Aerolineas Argentinas flight is now boarding. Farewell to the English-speaking world, and into the world of Spanish.

(*First published 9 September 2000.*)

2

Arriving

When I arrived in Santa María, a village in the *campo* (countryside) of Paraguay where I had chosen to spend a year, I was overwhelmed by its tranquillity and peace, just as I had been the first time I passed through the village in 1996. On that occasion I had drunk the water at the spring where the women go down to do their laundry in the open air. According to legend, those who drink of this water will return to Santa María. I am not superstitious, but I drank the water all the same.

Now, four years later, I came down to Santa María from Asunción by bus. I had been warned by the Sisters of the *Compañía de María*, who do pastoral work in the area, that it would be extremely difficult to rent anywhere in Santa María this year, because the nearby sugar factory was bringing in workers from all over the country. All rented accommodation, whether of rooms or houses, had gone.

Yet as the bus dropped me off onto Santa María's broad, red-earthed paths – no asphalt here – and as I walked up towards the white tower of the traditional church overlooking the spacious, tree-filled square, I felt again the same tug of affection for the place, and hoped that I would be able to stay.

Perhaps God was blessing my mission, for the one and only possibility that turned up was completely ideal for my needs. My little house – I can now say with pride – is built in the style typical of Paraguay, slim red bricks, covered with white rendering that is breaking off in places, and a sloping red-tiled roof. There is no glass in the windows, but wrought iron bars and mosquito netting, and the bedroom opens into the living room without an internal door. There is room for the four boxes of books I have brought and my various bits of journalistic technology, and one of the animators from the local Christian community is building me a bookcase. I have a flushing loo and a hot shower, where many of my neighbours only have a hole in the earth in an outside hut and a cold tap and bucket, but I cannot feel guilty about this since I had no other option. And I know that there are moments when you are ill or storms are raging, when roughing it stops being fun.

In the early morning there is a hullabaloo of cock-a-doodle-doos, and the sun rose this morning at 6.25 a.m. From my back door I can see it come up over the horizon of the lower slopes of a hill, and within five minutes everything that was covered in darkness is bathed in pink light. By day I am more likely to hear the creak of an ox cart outside my window, than a car. There is great quietness and simplicity: bright sunlight, red earth, and peace in the heart. Less than twelve hours later darkness falls again, almost as suddenly as it was lifted, and then the noise of Latin American music drifts from radios out of open doors and windows.

'The people here are very good,' I was assured by Carmencita, who lives in the main square and is involved with the Christian communities. 'There is nothing you need be afraid of, living alone. You can leave your door open all day, and no one will venture in or take anything.'

I greeted my neighbour Gregorio on the corner of the street the day I moved in. 'I am your new neighbour,' I said, and he clapped his hands with joy like a child. Delightful, if a little odd. The next day he seemed so different that at first I thought I must be speaking to someone else: he seemed, well, quite sober. And that proved to be the case: this gentleman is an alcoholic, I was told.

I was away for a few days in Asunción to follow the vice-presidential elections, and when I got back I heard Gregorio had died. Pneumonia was the official reason, and certainly it is easy to become sick in these chilly August days. (We are in the southern hemisphere.) There are so few cold days that no one is prepared for them, and there is no way of warming up when the cold strikes. But Gregorio's death was so sudden – he was walking down the street one day, and dead the next evening – that his metabolism must have been weakened.

I joined in the prayers for him in his house during the following octave. A staircase draped in white cloth and candles was placed against the wall, with ribbons leading up the nine steps to a cross at the top. Many friends and neighbours stood around it to pray the rosary, for despite his drinking, Gregorio was much loved by everyone as a good and kind neighbour. Amid these good people, who live in such poverty and yet know better than anyone how to love and pray and celebrate, I looked at those steps and knew that this place was indeed a stairway to heaven.

(*First published 9 September 2000.*)

ঙাঙ   ৪০৪০

There are now more cars than ox carts in Santa María, but there still are ox carts.

3

The square

I have one fear about writing about Santa María, and that is that it will be over-run by tourists. This may seem an unfounded fear, for I have yet to see a tourist here, even from Paraguay, let alone from another country or another continent. There ought to be a few, for we have a museum of outstanding wooden sculptures, carved when Santa María was one of the seventeenth-century Jesuit 'reductions' – or missions for the indigenous Guaraní, as in the film *The Mission*. The statues have been beautifully arranged in one of the original buildings of that period, with thick stone walls and heavy wooden beams, and it is a spiritual experience to walk into the sixth and final room, filled with depictions of Christ in his Passion.

The church, which is the next building, is a living extension of the museum, for it houses five more historic statues: a crucifix, a risen Christ, two angels with the broad brown faces of indigenous children, and the great Santa María de Fe itself (St Mary of Faith). Every Sunday night the church is filled with the music of a vigorous Mass in the Guaraní language, accompanied by guitar and harp – the traditional instrument of Paraguay, and possibly the most lovely instrument ever devised. Some of the hymns have been written by this local group, and the grandfather of one of the harpists wrote the setting for one of Paraguay's most famous songs, the *Pájaro Campana,* though it is said he never received the income he deserved for it. The kiss of peace is always a special moment, as *campesinos* embrace me with warm love, and we all sing *Dame la mano, Querido hermano* – 'Give me your hand, beloved brother/ sister'.

On the other side of the museum is the Sandy Bar, where my lovely friend Titina – who has a long black plait, few teeth, and ten grown-up children – cooks excellent lunches, and where the owner, Cayetana, is a fund of information. She told me about the day in 1974 when an art historian came to borrow the statue of Christ in Gethsemane for an exhibition in Brazil. He crated it up with great care, but by the time the lorry reached the far corner of the square the roads had become blocked by villagers, afraid to let their precious heritage go. He came back the next day with a police guard, but the people were ready and thronged around the church (where the statue was kept at that date) so that not even the police could force a way through. The statue remained in Santa María. The next year, with donations from the United States and Germany, work began on renovating the museum, to make a worthy home for it.

Another of Cayetana's accounts is of the five monkeys who live in the square and come down into her shop to steal her bread. Nobody knows how the first monkey arrived, but it was found in the trees, alone and frightened, by some children in 1995. Another monkey was then brought in from a nearby hill, in the hope that they would mate. Nothing happened, and eventually it was discovered that both were female. A third monkey was then brought in, a big black fellow, and there is now a happy family swinging through the tree tops. The square with its more than 150 trees is big enough to form a natural park for them, from which they have no desire to escape. Every time I walk through the square I look high up in the branches to search for them: they move around but always stay close to each other. And every walk through the streets brings me face to face with horses and cows grazing on the verges, not to mention the pigs, cocks, hens and dogs that also run around unfettered.

On the opposite side of the square from Cayetana's bar is the sewing workshop, which meets for three hours every afternoon to make colour-ful appliqué craftwork of typical scenes: women cooking over open fires, feeding the hens or carrying water on their heads; men riding on horse-back or working the fields. The income is shared equally between the members of the workshop, and earns them between 10p and 25p an hour, depending on sales. When I can, I join them, and the women laugh and joke in Guaraní as they sit around the table producing their wonderful creations. Last week my friend Demetria made everyone laugh as she told of the first time she went in a lift, seven years ago in Asunción; she was so alarmed that she clutched the hand of the next person, a young man, and was still clutching it tightly as she swayed out at the fifth floor with unreal, big steps as though walking onto the moon.

In this special and undiscovered place I feel an extraordinary sense of being at home, as though I am here because the person I love is here but I can never quite remember who that person is. (Can it be Jesus?) To come to Santa María I had to strip myself for a while of almost everything, including compatriots, language, family and employment, but in their place I have found not only art and music, culture and faith, but also the kind of love you learn from those who are poor and have nothing to lose.

(*First published 28 October 2000.*)

4

San Roque González

Paraguay 5, Peru 1. Paraguay's triumphant victory in the World Cup Qualifying rounds on 15 November 2000 was watched with jubilation here in Santa María. It was the first time I had seen the great goalie José Luis Chilavert in action, who cannot be confined to his goal but runs off down field and takes free kicks and penalties with blistering success. Football is a great leveller. This little, unknown country of Paraguay can now lift its head as the third great footballing nation of Latin America, after its bigger neighbours Argentina and Brazil.

But Paraguayans have surprisingly little sense of being Latin American, and my *campesino* friends are liable to ask me questions like 'Is Colombia in Europe?' The great Salvadorean saint awaiting canonisation, Romero of the Americas, is practically unheard of here. We have our own saint and martyr, San (that is, St) Roque González, whose feast also fell last week, on 17 November. The positive side of Pope John Paul's over-abundance of canonisations is that small nations now have their own saints, who boost the national sense of achievement just as much (well, almost as much) as a good football team.

I celebrated the feastday in San Antonio, one of the eleven outlying hamlets (or *compañías*) that form part of the municipality of Santa María. The priest from Santa María drives a jeep down the dirt track to say Mass in each of the *compañías* once a month, accompanied by a group of the Sisters who do most of the pastoral work. Confessions are heard before Mass – which is celebrated as evening falls, so as not to take people away from their work in the field while there is still light. Afterwards there is some sharing of food and visits to the sick, which can sometimes mean picking your way in pitch darkness to scattered cottages with no electricity.

It was a beautiful evening and San Roque González's feastday was marked by the baptism of some dozen children. The event was organised and overseen by the cheery laywoman who is animator of the local community. There were too many people to fit in the picturesque little church, so the Mass was celebrated outside, with the football pitch behind us and the white peeling walls and tower of the church as a backdrop.

Like our local priest today, Roque González was a Paraguayan Jesuit. The son of a Spanish conquistador and (almost certainly) an indigenous mother, he was born in Asunción in 1576, and joined the Jesuits, shortly after the province was established, with one over-riding desire – to evangelise among the indigenous. His initial task was to be the first missionary to the Guaycurú in the Chaco – a people so fierce that the Spanish said one Guaycurú was to be feared as much as 20 from any other tribe.

However, it was not at the hands of the Guaycurú that Roque González was to meet his fate, but in another area, nearly 20 years later. He had come to work in the Misiones region where I live today, becoming second Superior of the first Jesuit reduction – an economically self-sufficient settlement where the Guaraní were safe from slave-traders – and went on to found many other reductions, beginning each foundation with the planting of a cross. He denounced the exploitation of the indigenous by the Spanish, and insisted that the work of the Church could not be confined to the spiritual. 'We must be doctors not only of the soul,' he wrote, 'which is our principal role, but also of the body, attending them in their sicknesses and in their labour night and day.'

He translated a catechism into Guaraní, taught the indigenous to read, write and count, and supported the teaching of music, dance and singing which was so characteristic of the reductions. His energy was ceaseless. A Jesuit colleague wrote of him that 'one and the same person is carpenter, architect and bricklayer: he wields the axe, works the wood and carries it to the construction site, and he himself hooks up the yoke of oxen when there is no one else around. He does everything.' Roque González wrote to his Provincial of his labours, 'I am resolved to be here, though I should die a thousand deaths.' His death came in 1628 when he was fixing the clapper on a bell for a belltower: he was clubbed to death with a stone axe, on the instructions of a witchdoctor.

In this great tradition of missionary work Santa María still stands today (though there was rather more than a hiccup when the Jesuits were expelled in 1768, for they did not return to Paraguay until 1927). The cross of our 1647 foundation has been the subject of new building work this month, as a tastefully designed brick and tile shelter has been built to preserve it from the ravages of the weather.

(*First published 25 November 2000.*)

5

Santa María's terrible memories

Today is 24 March 2001, the twenty-first anniversary of the killing of Archbishop Oscar Romero, who was shot dead as he said Mass in a hospital chapel in San Salvador. As I have been preparing a lecture on Romero 'seen through Paraguayan eyes', I decided the time had come to talk to people tortured in the Stroessner years – the 35-year dictatorship that ended only in 1989. It would not need much more than a puff of wind for those days to return, given the number of Stroessner's former ministers or their relatives who have come back into government.

I walked to Santa María's leafy square to look for Victor, who plays the accordion at Mass, while his 20-year-old son Isabelino is lead guitarist. Victor was sitting outside his house mending a neighbour's car radio, and he cleared a space for me to sit down. I began by asking about Bishop Bogarín, who died 25 years ago, and who has been described to me as a saint – strong and forthright in denouncing injustice and human-rights abuses, a defender of the poor. Appropriately, he was an indirect descendant of San Roque González.

'Some say', I proposed, 'that Monsenor Bogarín died as something of a martyr himself, from grief and anxiety. It was a heart attack, but people say his house was just across the road from the cells where they used to torture people, and he would lie awake and hear their screams.' Victor confirmed this, and, without taking his eyes off the wires and screw-driver, began to tell me about his own torture.

He had been involved with a movement called JAC (*Juventud Agraria Cristiana*, Agrarian Christian Youth) and they had a piece of land to farm in common. This was said by Stroessner's men to be communism, as was also a cooperative which enabled them to buy food in bulk at cheaper prices. For Stroessner, he said, three people constituted a meeting, and meetings were banned. People in Santa María did not even dare go to church. At Mass there would be two old women, one of them blind and the other her ancient stepmother, plus a couple of children.

At 8.00 am on 5 April 1976 Victor was arrested while he was working in the fields, and marched home at riflepoint to collect his clothes. At 3.00 am the following night he was taken to the torture chamber. First there were beatings with a whip, and then the electricity. Victor took the wires from the car radio and wrapped one round his thumb and another round his little finger to show how they did it. They would sit him on a chair with a metal base, with a helmet to enclose his head. He demon-strated with the other hand the way they would wind a handle fast to send the current through his body: 'rrrmm, rrrmm, rrrmm'. They would go on until he was nearly dead, and then they would stop, and then start again. They wanted to know all the details of his activity – whom he was with, what he was doing – but there was not anything to say, only about the common land and the common store, nothing else.

Then there were other tortures, such as being submerged in a bath, or being hung upside down, or stuffed down the sewers. Victor was tortured every day for three months, and fed on rotten food with maggots in it. Then he was taken to a prison in Asunción. This first imprisonment lasted two years and six months, and he had two subsequent periods in jail.

Isabelino saw me talking to his father and came out with great warmth to greet me. 'We are talking about grave matters,' I said, unable to return his happy smile. Victor asked Isabelino to point to the scar under his chin where the point of a knife had been pressed, in order to make him sign a confession he had no part in producing. The United States would pay money for every captured communist, they alleged, and this was how the numbers were faked.

Then Isabelino, who was in nursery school during his father's last imprisonment, spoke of the isolation he suffered throughout his childhood because people were afraid to have anything to do with his family. I could never have guessed that someone so lively and intelligent, so dynamic and talented, could have been a companion to so much pain.

Both father and son were matter of fact and unemotional in their account. The crickets chirped, and the square was filled with peace. But the romantic red earth of Paraguay was showing a new aspect. Could it be that it was not red from its iron content, but rather stained with blood?

(*First published 24 March 2001.*)

6

Pascua Dolorosa

The theme of Victor's torture recurred this month in Santa María, for this Holy Week 2001 marked the twenty-fifth anniversary of the most savage period of Stroessner's repression of the early basic Christian communities, known as *Ligas Agrarias Cristianas* (Christian Agrarian Leagues). Santa María was one of seven parishes in the Misiones region to hold a commemorative ceremony.

On Wednesday of Holy Week I went round to the house of Eliodoro Coronel, who is always known by the nickname Patrón, though as a humble *campesino* he is not too keen on its meaning of 'boss'. He is one of the Christian community animators and a eucharistic minister. More than that, he is one of Santa María's torture survivors.

It was a hot day and he met me with his brown body stripped to the waist and the local iced drink of *tereré* in his hand: 'At last I can welcome you to my house,' he said. I gave him and his artistic wife Není a little prayer card in commemoration of Wednesday of Holy Week 1976, when he was first arrested. In Paraguay the custom of Holy Wednesday is to cook *chipas* – a roll made from maize flour – in the traditional outdoor oven known as a *tatakua* – a 'fire-hole' in Guaraní. It is brick-built and shaped like a small igloo: you light a wood fire inside and when the bricks are really hot you take out the fire and put your food in to cook from the powerful residual heat. The *chipas* are for eating on Good Friday, when no cooking must be done. It may seem odd to prepare them two days in advance, but on Maundy Thursday people are busy cooking a midday roast, and in the evening the celebrations of the Passion begin.

On Holy Wednesday evening in 1976, Patrón had just finished helping Není put the *chipas* in to cook when the police arrived and tried to entice him away with a lie about a neighbour needing an injection. Then they produced a gun and he agreed to leave his house quietly so as not to alarm the children. They tied his hands and bundled him into a jeep, where they offered him whisky. He said he did not drink and they said that in any case they would not have given him any because he was a 'communist'. On Good Friday he was tortured, as Jesus was, with a whip tipped with a steel ball, until he was bleeding all over.

This year, Patrón was one of those closest to the tabernacle during the late-night vigil of Maundy Thursday. It was very much a community occasion, with hymns and readings and the sharing of reflections and prayers, and after keeping silent for a long time, Patrón spoke of the· *Pascua Dolorosa* of 1976 – the sorrowful Easter. Then we stood together around the tabernacle and said the Lord's Prayer, and went out into the night.

The crucifix that was unveiled for veneration the next afternoon was two centuries old, a work of art from the period of the reductions. It is the most beautiful crucifix I have ever had the privilege of kissing on Good Friday. 'What are these men thinking?' I wondered, as I watched both Victor and Patrón out of the corner of my eye during the reading of the Passion.

On Holy Saturday morning there was a commemoration of the *Pascua Dolorosa*, with a dramatisation of *campesinos* being torn away from their families, and teachers from their schools. Patrón was one of those who stood up and spoke of his experiences, and Victor was another. Victor's son Isabelino presented the event, which was broadcast over the diocesan station, Radio San Roque González.

But Holy Week was painful not only because of its memories of the past: it also brought its own fresh suffering – two motorbike accidents. On uneven dirt roads pitted with holes, with rickety bridges and no road signs, motorbikes are more than usually dangerous, but the poor have no other means of transport, other than horseback and the very rare bus.

Both victims were teachers, travelling to and from their work – Miriam, a young mother, who fought with death under intensive care, and is now on the slow path to recovery with multiple fractures; and Isabelino himself, who accompanies adult *campesinos* taking part in a radio school, and for whom this is the third accident on his vehicle. With his agonising leg plunged in a bucket of iced water he joked to me: 'At this rate it will be a miracle if I reach 40.' But it is not actually funny.

Rather, this is another way in which the poor offer their lives for their sisters and brothers. In this Easter season, as I receive communion from Patrón, or from our Jesuit priest, Vicente Barreto, another torture survivor, I feel myself richly privileged to live through the paschal mystery with people who have withstood so much suffering for love of Christ. It is a wealth that money cannot buy.

(*First published 28 April 2001.*)

ඥඥ   ඪඪ

For more about Miriam's accident, see chapter 8, 'Miriam' (p.21).

7

Protest at the sugar factory

'Nothing like this has ever happened before in Santa María,' said
Demetria, jubilant after the 400-strong march in support of the local
sugar-factory workers who have been temporarily laid off, two of her
sons among them. There is no dole in Paraguay. The local economy is
close to collapse and the workers are deep in debt. They were promised
their jobs back after three months – the length of time you can leave an
electricity bill unpaid without being cut off – but that period has expired
and the factory remains closed.

It was a classic Latin American demo: strong, loud, and peaceable. The
people gathered behind banners and national flags among the trees of
the square, looking determined and disciplined. Then they were off
around the streets, with united cries of '*Obreros, unidos, jamás serán
vencidos*' ('Workers, united, will never be defeated') and the singing of
'*Patria querida, somos tu esperanza*' ('Beloved country, we are your
hope'). There were the usual explosions of fire crackers, and an impres-
sively dignified singing of the national anthem.

But more impressive even than the march is the encampment outside
the factory gates, that has been going on now for nearly two weeks, with
regular numbers of between fifty and a hundred, despite the fact that it is
a half-hour walk from Santa María, and the weather has been at times

bitterly cold. Men, women and children chat, cook, plot and are simply present as a protest, informally grouped around two large orange and green tarpaulin tents.

I have watched the sugar factory off and on since last September, when I went to an open day to see the machines, receive a tiny packet of organic sugar and hear from the management how the factory was run. This was the only factory in the country, I was told, that produced exclusively organic sugar. The employees worked an 8-hour day, and anything above that was overtime. But there was one give-away phrase that made me probe further: 'We have no trade-union problems here.' But surely there is a trade union, I enquired? There is none needed, the management told me, because the boss is so receptive to the workers' concerns.

The next day I met with some workers and heard a very different story. Nearly everyone worked a 12-hour day, seven days a week, with three weeks of day work followed by a week of nights, admittedly with over-time pay. People went into work however ill they might be, because they were afraid of losing their jobs. Anyone who was dismissed had no means of enquiring or protesting, for they would not even be allowed inside the gate. And since the factory was virtually the only local employer, there were always people queuing up to take their places. Everyone wanted a trade union but no one had had the courage to start one, because, they said, the boss did not want one.

The suspension of work came like a bolt from the blue in January, when the management decided to cut costs by employing its workers only during the six months or so of the sugar-cane season, and suddenly announced it had no money to pay wages. The workers had two weeks' notice, and were stunned, outraged, but powerless. A meeting was con-voked, however, and the boss signed with them an agreement that the suspension would last just three months.

The workers thought this was the best deal they could get, but they felt later they had been tricked. Not only did the factory remain closed after the three months were up, but they also discovered that the management had to receive permission from the Ministry for Justice and Work for the 90-day suspension, and that the Ministry had rejected the application. Had the workers not already signed a document in the presence of a justice of the peace, the management would have had no legitimate grounds for suspending their contracts.

But the dispute has had one good effect: it has provoked the formal setting up of a trade union. With the union's organisation there has been a series of public meetings, marches, and even – because this is Latin America – parties. Demetria has been one of the most vocal. 'Our form of celebration', she proclaimed to the crowd, 'is to meet together to claim our rights, as people who are humble and poor. And who else is humble and poor among us? Jesus, who came into the world to share our life.'

At the encampment on Mothers' Day (15 May) the occasional passing motorists donated money, cakes, rice and pasta to keep the campfires occupied and the stomachs filled. The music of guitars and accordions filled the air, Paraguayan flags fluttered in the breeze, dogs wandered, children played, men and women danced. There was a great sense that this spot by the roadside was the only place to be, and one could only feel sorry for any management who would have to make their lonely way through the fun to get to the forbidden grounds of the factory within.

(*First published 26 May 2001.*)

ೞೞ   ౸౸

When the factory eventually reopened, all the trade union leaders lost their jobs: if not directly sacked, they were forced out by more subtle means. Those lucky enough to be given work there now found they were being paid up to three months late. And there were a huge number of industrial accidents, usually of the metal-splinter-in-the-eye variety, though there was also a case of a worker trapped in a machine who had both his legs sliced off. The sugar factory was taken over in 2011 by an international investment group and there are high hopes that it may turn into a positive benefit for the people. Hopes of a new management have been raised and dashed before, but this time we think it is for real.

8

Miriam

The little room with a cement floor and bare brick walls was thronged with *campesinos*, standing around a double bed on which lay a beautiful young woman flat on her back. Her right leg was bent and encased in plaster. Her left leg – the worse of the two – was covered in scars. Her face had the sad resignation of someone who had had nothing to do for the last four months but stare at the ceiling.

Miriam was the victim of a motorbike accident in Holy Week, on her way home for lunch after teaching in school. She was now back in her family home for a couple of weeks before being returned to hospital in Asunción to have the plaster removed and – if the money can be found – to have her sixth operation, which would involve a prosthesis for her left femur and knee and would open the way for her to walk again.

The *campesinos* around the bed were members of the Christian community visiting the sick after their weekly meeting, with their tiny offering of money. They sang with her a hymn that included the line, 'On the road there is always someone wounded, who needs my help and my friendship'. They joined hands and prayed the *Ore Ru* ('Our Father' in Guaraní) and the room was filled with the fervour of prayer from those who want to give so much more than their material circumstances permit.

I first heard of Miriam's accident on 10 April from my neighbour as she was hanging out her washing to dry on her barbed wire fence. I did not at first realize this was the Miriam I knew, the daughter-in-law of my friend Candé and the mother of a 4-year-old son. The news on that first day was so grim that everyone thought she would die. Her motorbike had suffered a full frontal smash with a jeep that, according to the reports, was travelling around a blind bend on the wrong side of the dirt road and at excessive speed.

The jeep belonged to a Coronel Aristides Ayala, a supporter of some-time coup-leader Lino Oviedo, but it was being driven by his law-student son Eduardo Aristides. When there is such a combination of back-grounds, in the army and the law, *campesinos* feel helpless about getting any financial compensation: people with footholds in the corridors of power can manipulate or bribe their way out of any awkward corner, and the concept of equality before the law is a farce. The Ayala family has offered one thousand pounds as a final settlement, but Miriam's first operation alone cost nearly twice that, and her husband Jose Miguel had to mortgage the house to pay for it. If the family cannot recover what they have already paid out for the five operations, they will be left homeless. And if they cannot raise a further four thousand pounds for this sixth operation, Miriam may never walk again.

The first thing that Jose Miguel knew of the accident was when, by chance, he travelled along the same route in a friend's car and recognized his wife's smashed-up motorbike. 'Oh my God,' he said, 'Miriam must be dead.' But she had been taken to the health centre moaning in her brief flashes of consciousness, 'What has happened to me? Why are my legs hurting so much?' From there she was taken into intensive care and four young men from Santa María went down to the hospital to donate blood for her.

When I saw Candé on the day of the accident we hugged each other in silent grief. I thought of the little boy and the likelihood that he would be left motherless, and could find no words. He meanwhile was wandering around hand-in-hand with Candé's youngest daughter in a daze, not knowing what was going on.

But Miriam did not die. I visited her in hospital two months after her accident and was shocked by what I saw. Her poor legs were flopped motionless onto pillows and peppered with the most ugly and multiple scars. Her pelvis had been broken open, she had screws in her side, she could not raise her left arm, and eating caused her great pain. My pathetic gift of tangerines sat useless at the side of her bed. Almost the only part of her that was intact and healthy was her brain.

I sat by Miriam's bed again in Santa María as she did an interview for local radio. When she was asked how she felt about being separated for so long from her little boy she broke down, and the interviewer had to fill in for several minutes before she could find words again.

(*First published 20 September 2001.*)

ତ୨ତ୨   ৪৩৪৩

Thanks to the generosity of Tablet *readers, over £12,000 was raised, which more than covered Miriam's medical costs.*

9

Who rules the world?

'You cannot fight terrorism with terrorism,' said our parish priest at Mass last Sunday. 'We must pray for the conversion of heart of those attacking Afghanistan.' If this was said in a church in Britain, it might cause a storm of protest. In Santa María, there was not a ripple. What Vicente Barreto had said in the wake of the Twin Towers incident was regarded as obvious.

After 11 September there was universal sympathy for the innocent civilians in the United States. But when bereavement turned to fighting talk and then to military action, sympathy here was replaced by a more familiar sense of resentment at the way the United States rules the world. Particularly resented was President Bush's threat that those who were not with the United States in their fight were on the side of the terrorists. The Jesuit magazine *Acción* – more or less *The Tablet*'s opposite number in Paraguay – ran an article that called that declaration 'so monumentally ridiculous that it will go down in history as a shameful model of imperialism'. No one can say that, maintained the author, 'without being himself a terrorist!'

Does everyone in Paraguay think this? There is always a variety of views. In an opinion poll on the Humberto Rubín political discussion programme of Telefuturo, 28 per cent agreed with the attacks against

Afghanistan, and 79 per cent opposed them. A student in Asunción told me that among his contacts 'most people don't have an opinion, but of those who do, it's a small group of extremists who take the side of the United States – basically people with contacts at the Embassy, or friends or family living in the States.'

The most prominent supporter of the United States' action in Afghanistan is President González Macchi. Why should he take a position that does not represent the views of his people? 'Out of fear,' people tell me, 'it stands to reason.' And when I think about it, anyone responsible for the lives and well-being of five million Paraguayans would indeed do well not to have the United States class the country as 'on the side of the terrorists'.

After all, Latin America has lived through a whole generation of blood and tears, with many more than 6,000 deaths, as a result of the United States' fight against what they chose to label in a similarly Humpty Dumpty way as 'communism'. 'All the dictatorships in Latin America', said a doctor friend of mine in Asunción, 'were shored up by the United States: Paraguay's, Chile's, Bolivia's, Brazil's, Argentina's, Uruguay's … 'And that is before you even get out of the Southern Cone, let alone into Central America. People who have seen their countries mucked up by US foreign policy are not surprised to see attacks being made on the headquarters of military power in Washington, and on the symbol of economic domination in New York, however disapproving they may be of killing 6,000 innocent people in the process.

At the Triple Frontier of Paraguay, Brazil and Argentina, the inhabitants are forming an organisation called Peace Without Frontiers to defend themselves against the accusation by the United States that they are a zone of Muslim extremists funding terrorism. People of 57 ethnic origins have lived in the region 'in harmony for more than 100 years without a single act of discrimination or terrorism', they maintain, as they prepare a demonstration for 11 November featuring the release of doves and balloons.

What do ordinary *campesinos* think? They are generally a nonjudgmental lot, free of the critical edge that marks those with more international experience. I asked a group of base-community animators visiting Santa María what they thought about the war, as they sat in a circle on benches at our medicinal garden. There was a pause in the quiet heat of midday before a woman answered.

'What strikes me most', she said, 'is the arrogance.' 'Arrogance on which side?' I asked. 'Well on both sides,' she said, 'but I was thinking in particular of a US Peace Corps volunteer who lives in our village, and who talks about how his country is going to win this war because they are the most powerful country in the world. There is a war-like spirit there, and to hear him going on about it is very ugly.'

Then a man spoke. 'What I find worst is the killing of innocent people,' he said. 'Innocent people on which side?' I asked. 'Well, both sides,' he said, 'but what I was thinking about most was the people suffering the bombardments in Afghanistan.'

I turned to the Jesuit novice master who had brought the *campesinos* to visit us. 'What are people saying in your house?' I asked. Almost reluctantly he told me, 'The first comment in our house after 11 September came from the cook, who said, "Now the United States is suffering in its own flesh the kind of suffering they have been inflicting for so long on other countries around the world." ' He added sadly, 'But it does not justify it. It does not justify it.'

10

Funeral

November is the month of the dead, and this November has seen the death of my neighbour's brother, at the age of 68, a couple of weeks after he was sent home from hospital with inoperable cancer. The custom is to have a night vigil, so he was buried on the following morning. To wait longer is impossible in a hot country, and we are now approaching 40 degrees. Between the death and the funeral, the body remains all the time in the house and the relatives and friends gather there to pray.

I went to pay my respects in the afternoon, crossing the football pitch to a pretty white house where all the doors were open to let the air blow through. On a table immediately in front of the door was the open coffin surrounded by flowers and candles, and the rosary was in full session. The body was clothed in a white robe and white girdle, and there was a transparent white muslin cloth over the face so that the only parts that could be clearly seen were the two hands, as yellow and opaque as a wax work.

The relatives were standing a pace back from the coffin, repetitively murmuring the responses and wiping away the odd tear, some of them with the deadpan look that comes to people who are very tired and have to keep going. The daughter by contrast – a woman in her late forties dressed in a black trouser suit – was leaning directly over the coffin, hugging the body and letting her tears plop down over it.

When the rosary came to an end, the visitors who were crowding the doorway came in to touch the coffin and cross themselves, and to embrace the chief mourners. There was much noise of sobbing, but none so loud as the daughter who began to scream 'Papá', now falling into the arms of an aunt for comfort, now turning back to the body and tearing off the muslin veil as though she hoped to caress the face back into life. But it was as hard and solid as a block of wood, and as she struggled to embrace the body, I could see how the ribcage fell away beneath the white robe into an emaciated stomach.

The next morning at the cemetery the display of grief was even more dramatic. Before being taken to the tomb the coffin was placed on a slab before a cross, and the widow and daughter, four brothers, five sisters and their families, stood still and expectant under a huddle of black brollies against the sun. Then the lid of the coffin was lifted just a little so they could catch their last glimpse of the body, and the quiet, serious group was instantly transformed into a hubbub. Women howled and fought fiercely with their menfolk, who were having to pull them forcibly away from the body and hold back their flailing limbs.

As the coffin was carried through the muddle of graves and tombs there were noisy sounds of sobbing from all around in the stumbling crowd. The family tomb was a big square slab and a hole had been opened in the front so the coffin could be slid in. Like Hamlet at the funeral of Ophelia, several relatives made as if to be buried alive with it, and were carried away, struggling hysterically and crying out words blurred with distress. The local equivalent of a gravedigger was a brick-layer, who bricked up the space rapidly before there could be any more attempts of suicidal folly. My neighbour Adela was one of those who collapsed with grief and had to be firmly helped away.

A couple of hours later she came round to my house to thank me for a little prayer card I had slipped into her hands at the wake. I asked how she was feeling and she told me, 'A bit better now. We are all so grateful that he died quickly, without suffering too much. Once we were told that there was no cure we prayed that he would soon be at rest.' I told her funeral customs were very different in my country, where people show little outward grief but later suffer long-term bereavement depression from their suppressed feelings. 'Not here,' she said, 'here we let it out, and then we feel better afterwards.'

What a contrast with my own culture where people run away from death by sending people to hospital to die, and never bring them home again to where they belong. The corpses are shut away into discreet morgues, hermetically sealed into coffins by experts at handling dead bodies, slid mechanically behind curtains to canned music, and hygienically turned into ashes: out of sight and into the unconscious.

But my over-riding thought was of how this person, in all his deathly ugliness, was so extraordinarily loved. Yet this was just an ordinary funeral, like any other. Death is a time of blessing if it reveals that there is so much love in the world.

(*First published 24 November 2001.*)

11

Bullfight

Leandro and Basilia have lost their cow, electrocuted on the fence surrounding the police station. It was worth a million and a half guaraníes. That is not as much as it sounds (actually £230) but it is still almost their entire livelihood. She was a fine cow, a very good milker, who produced seven litres a day. At 15 pence a litre this enabled them to live in dignity.

'But I don't understand it,' I said. 'In my country the electric fences are not so highly charged as to kill animals who touch them.'

People tell me, 'Well, it was raining.'

'I suppose they did not have insurance?' I asked. Stupid question. No one here has insurance for anything, not even for cars. This is partly because 90 per cent of the valuables people have are contraband or stolen property (or so I am told, with perhaps a touch of exaggeration). Not so, Leandro and Basilia's cow. But with £1.05 a day income, who could afford insurance?

Basilia was upset when I went round. 'We are poor, and she was a lovely cow,' she told me. If that was said by the English it would mean she was a pretty colour, had a gentle temperament and was known by a pet name. Not so here. It referred only to her milk production. My friends think the English are soft in the head to give names to their animals.

'Is there nothing to be done?' I asked. 'Nothing,' she said. 'The police say it is illegal to keep a cow in a populated area.' If there is such a rule, no one knows it and no one keeps it: the pretty red-earth-and-green-grass streets are scattered with grazing cows. The only objections come from the dogs, who regard it as a point of honour to bark furiously and chase them away from their property at full pelt. The first time I saw a cow being chased along the road at the speed of a cantering horse I was shocked that the dog's owners did not reproach their pet. Another soft-in-the-head English reaction. I soon found all dogs do the same.

I bought some eggs from Basilia and ordered a chicken for the next day. Leandro seemed cheered by my arrival when I went back, and tested me out on my Guaraní. He is a talented musician – one of our two harpists in church, and one of the few men who regularly attends the Christian community meetings. As for Basilia, she takes part in a Christian work community producing cheap soap and detergents, which are sold in old fizzy-drink bottles.

She now came out of the kitchen with a huge chicken in a plastic bag, freshly prepared. I have learned that one has to specify preparation when ordering poultry. Once when I bought a duck I was asked how I would like it. 'What do you mean?' I asked. They meant did I want it dead or alive. 'Well, dead of course, I am going to eat it,' I said. Ah, but many people would buy it alive, I was told, so they could kill it just before eating and have it at maximum freshness.

Cows here look different from British cows. They are heavier and uglier and have more loose skin hanging down from their throats. Often they have a forked branch tied round their necks to stop them pushing their way through fences, which makes them look even clumsier. The ungainly quality is especially notable with the bulls, and when there are bullfights, the aim is not to kill the bull but to make it fall down, which makes it look even more ungainly. The men will leap on the bull, pull its tail really hard and wrap their legs round the bull's legs, until it falls over. Then everyone claps. I feel even more sorry for these bulls than I do for the noble Spanish creatures that spill their blood on the sand. Paraguayan bulls are made to look ridiculous.

What am I doing going to bullfights? Well, I go to look at the people – the tight, buzzing crowd piled steeply into overflowing banks of benches, an extraordinary concentration of lively Latin American culture. But last time I went, the people looked at me instead.

What happened was that the bull won. It could not be toppled. A whole group of men all tried at the same time to make it fall over, pushing and shoving and tugging and tripping, but they failed. Eventually the bull was allowed out of the ring. Hurray for the bull, I thought, breaking into enthusiastic applause for the first bull ever to have been victorious over its tormentors. My claps were the only sound to be heard. Every face turned to stare disapprovingly at this ill-educated woman who was applauding human failure. I looked at my watch and decided I had better be off to bed.

When I told my friends afterwards, some thought it very funny. Others were evidently shocked. It was as if I had gone to a gymnastic display and applauded when people fell flat on their faces. The kinder ones said, 'You got it the wrong way round: you are meant to clap the men not the bulls.' I have not been to a bullfight since.

(*First published 2 February 2002.*)

12

Scholarships

It is back to school time in Paraguay, after the long summer holiday. Shops are full of pencils, pens and stacks of exercise books. Pupils who did not pass their exams in December are sitting their re-takes to permit them to pass into the next year. Some are in despair because they owe fees and are not permitted to sit their exams. This tough but necessary rule weighs most heavily, of course, on those in tertiary education.

Earlier this month I went to visit the *Directora* of the Universidad Católica in neighbouring San Ignacio. She showed me a list of students from Santa María with economic problems. There were a dozen, a third of them still with fees outstanding, which means that they cannot pass into the next year and may never be able to finish their studies. I have a little money in the Santa Maria Education Fund which I started, and I hoped it would be enough to help at least one student over this year's hump.

'You see this file on my desk?' she said. 'It is full of applications from students for discounts on their fees.' She explained: 'At the Universidad Católica in Asunción and in Encarnación the students tend to come from professional families and can pay, but here the population is very different. Everyone struggles, and we help as best we can, but every half-scholarship is money that the University loses. Yet we have to offer them because otherwise we would have no students.'

33

The next day I went to visit Elida and Justina Uliambre who are studying, respectively, Law and Pedagogy, and who between them owed £170. They live in the countryside a good half-hour's walk away from my house, and the parish priest gave me a lift in his jeep. The girls' father, Saturnino Uliambre, is a hero of the *Ligas Agrarias Cristianas* which Stroessner savagely repressed. He spent two years in prison and was tortured. I like the idea of one of his daughters becoming a lawyer, to build a new generation of justice and hope. And I like it especially because the university tells me she is an outstanding student.

I know how I used to feel when I lived in the developed North: I knew how important it was to help people from poor and marginalized backgrounds to come forward as new leaders in society, but the difficult challenge was to find the right young people with the talent and the will to complete their studies and get qualified. Here on the ground in Paraguay, that feels the easy bit. The difficult bit is to find the money.

The poverty of the Uliambre family is evident. We sat outside their little house, which had seen the upbringing of ten children, and drank the local drink of *tereré*, without ice, which is almost unheard of but indicates that they are too poor to have a fridge in this sweltering country. Justina is quiet but bright-eyed and attentive, Elida talkative in a thoughtful way.

'People told me not to go into law, because it is a corrupt profession,' she said, 'and yet I think I will be able to do something.' They were pursuing their studies as an act of faith, with encouragement from the bishop and occasional contributions of money from their elder brother who is working elsewhere. They did not know when more money would arrive, nor how much it would be, but had a quiet determination that they would get through their education somehow, in the end.

The following day I searched out another law student called Fredy, which was easier as he lives three blocks from my home, in a small, simple house with a very well tended garden. I asked if the financial difficulties with the university had been resolved. 'In no way,' said Fredy's mother, as they told me their story. Fredy's father works in a metal factory in Buenos Aires, but with the economic collapse of Argentina he now works only half the week, and is paid for only half the time he works, while the peso has sunk to half its former value. If you work that out it means the family of seven are existing on something like one-eighth of their former income. So I cleared Fredy's debt and he can sit his exams.

Whatever the discounts that can be offered, it will always be a small number of students from here who are able to go to the Universidad Católica. To offer tertiary education to a larger number of the poor there is a new Institute of further education in Santa María which is training people to qualify in food technology. It seems to be a profession needed in the countryside where food is grown and where there is at present only one qualified food technologist in the whole department of Misiones. The Institute began shortly after I arrived (but was not founded by me), and it has been run on something less than a shoestring, with no pay for the teachers, no rent for the dangerously tumbledown building, and fees of less than £5 a month. That is still too much for most to pay, but with help from the Santa Maria Education Fund the Institute is going to be able to offer full scholarships this year to many of its students.

Emi, who is in charge of the finances, came round to my house one night, to 'share a doubt' with me. She talked around the subject of the Institute and the new building they need. The plan at the time was that the building would be constructed with volunteer labour. Finally I pressed her, 'What is your doubt?' She said, 'It's that you won't be able to find the money to buy the building materials.'

I told her, 'I'm not at all worried about that. My doubt is a different one. It's that you won't be able to find the volunteers for the labour.' She assured me, 'I'm not at all worried about that.' 'Well then,' I said, 'you must give me your confidence on the labour, and I must give you my confidence on the money. It's like St Paul's idea of the body of Christ: the hand needs the foot and the foot needs the hand. Together we can make it.'

(*First published 2 March 2002.*)

13

Climbing the hill on Good Friday

People in Santa María do not talk much about Easter, but they talk a great deal about Holy Week. 'My son is coming home for Holy Week,' they say, not 'My son is coming home for Easter.'

There are no Easter eggs here, and no Easter bunnies, thank God, but Santa María lives its own form of struggle between sacred and secular, even though to my eyes the whole place seems drenched in devotion compared to where I have come from. Palm Sunday is picturesque. All the stay-at-home Catholics come out for it, bearing elaborate ornaments of greenery, with palm fronds plaited together and bent around to make baskets or other displays. They gather in the centre of Santa María's shady square, carrying their tall green bouquets along with little bottles of water, and the idea is that the water is blessed and will last them through the year, as something they can splash around the house during a storm to invoke divine protection. Is this a lovely folk expression of the faith, or pagan superstition pegging itself onto the Christian story?

Thursday is the great feast, just as the Last Supper was for Jesus. And so the barbecued joint of Maundy Thursday is more special than the Easter dinner – which is most likely eating up the remains of Thursday's cold meat. I still have difficulty adjusting to the huge quantities that Paraguay-ans eat when they have a roast, for meat is so cheap here that it does not make sense to stint on it. While you are still struggling through one great hunk on your plate someone will come along and change it for another. 'Try this piece, it's hot, and the other is getting cold,' they will say.

The right blend of bittersweet celebration and sorrow in Holy Week is an elusive business, hard to grasp and harder to get right, just as elusive and bewildering as it was on the original Palm Sunday, when the Hosannas rang out for the King who was to die. So there was conflict last Maundy Thursday night between the churchgoers, who watched with heavy hearts before the tabernacle, and the clientele of the *Cielo* bar at the corner of the square, where they celebrated heartily into the early hours. It so annoyed the parish priest that he made a public denunciation the next day. He is undoubtedly right on the offensive nature of carousing while Jesus is under arrest. And there is considerable sensitivity to that here, for people vividly and fondly remember the custom – sadly discontinued – of banning church bells from Maundy Thursday night to Easter, and using a rattle instead to summon people to church.

Good Friday has a very special custom in Santa María, which is that everyone walks to the *Cerro*. This is a small hill more than an hour's walk away but still in the municipality of Santa María, and there are stations of the cross leading up to the tiny rounded peak with its three crosses. People set off very early in the morning, at 5.00, 4.00 or even 3.00 am, to avoid the heat of the sun, and once on the peak they hang around and chatter, packing in ever more thickly as more crowds arrive, until there is hardly room to find a square metre of rock to sit down upon. A little group squeeze into a tiny chapel to say the rosary, and another little group stop to pray at the stations on the way up, but the great majority just make it a day outing, looking at the view, meeting their friends, and maybe buying a little ice cream if they can afford it.

Is this a good Good Friday or a bad Good Friday? I understand the hesitations of those who say that for most of the youth it is not a pilgrimage but a party. But what I like about it is that it is a physical exercise, a penitential exercise, even if not conducted in a very evident spirit of penance. An hour's walk, a steep climb, a hill in memory of Calvary … What better way to keep Good Friday?

Walking after all is a great sign of poverty and penance, and lack of transport is one of the harshest dividing marks between the haves and the have-nots. My friend Lourdes and her young children walk in to

Santa María every day – sometimes twice a day – from the *compañía* of Trinidad Kue, along the same route that leads to the *Cerro*. Each journey takes an hour and a half, and there is only one bicycle between the family.

'But isn't there a bus to get the children to school?' I asked her. 'Yes,' she said, 'but we do not have the money for the fare.' The fare is 23p. It is not a bad idea to experience that walk of hers at least once a year, as a reminder.

There is a hymn that is sung much here, especially in processions, which gathers together and blesses the walking of the poor. It is better in Spanish, but you get the idea in English:

> Mary of the walkers, teach us to walk.
> We are pilgrims, but it is difficult to keep going.
>
> You made a long walk to attend to Elizabeth.
> Knowing that you were God's dwelling place, you said 'Yes' to Gabriel.
>
> Yours was a humble walk, in the company of Jesus,
> When you walked through the villages, sharing his light.

> *María de los caminantes,*
> *Enséñanos a caminar.*
> *Nosotros somos peregrinos,*
> *Pero es difícil siempre andar.*
>
> *Hiciste larga caminada,*
> *Para servir a Isabel,*
> *Sabiéndote de Dios morada,*
> *Dijiste 'Sí' a Gabriel.*
>
> *Humilde fue tu caminada,*
> *En compañía de Jesús,*
> *Cuando andaba por los pueblos,*
> *Compartiendo de su luz.*

(*First published 30 March 2002.*)

14

At knifepoint in Asunción

One of my new ventures is to teach a Biblical course at our Institute in Santa María, and to prepare for my classes I was on my way this Wednesday to the Universidad Católica in Asunción to see if I could read in the library. The bus stopped one block away, and I was walking along the pavement by the outside fence of the Católica to reach the gate. It was four o'clock in the afternoon.

Just ahead of me a young man standing by a tree turned around and got in my way. There was nothing hostile or aggressive in his face or his movements, but I saw that in his hand there was a knife. I turned back, only to find another man blocking me from behind. They seized the handbag that I always carry with a long strap crossed around my body: I have no idea now if they pulled it off or cut if off, but I found myself crying out in English, 'What do you want? What do you want?', willing to give them anything but my life. Then I was on the ground with the knife threatening my body. I prepared myself for the stabs with a sense of unreality, saying to myself 'This is not really happening,' and then, 'Oh yes, it is.'

I had eyes only for the knife, and as I struggled to elude it I eventually realised that what they were aiming at was my body belt, where I keep my mobile phone and small change. So I kept still and let them bring the knife close to my body to slice slickly through the belt. They did it with the air of professionals undertaking an unpleasant but necessary task. Then they were off with their takings. I did not even want to watch where they went. I only wanted them to disappear.

I got to my feet and ran inside the compound, where the people in the office helped with my most immediate and urgent needs, which were paper and pen, and a little money to get back to the house where I was staying. They did not look encouraging at the idea that the police might be able to assist. When there is robbery in Paraguay, the police are often involved, being paid a cut of the takings to keep quiet. Last week there was a robbery at the nearest bank to Santa María, and when the alarm sounded the police turned up, walked around the building, said, 'We cannot see anything', and went back to their police station again.

All the same, the office at the Católica rang the police, and four officers arrived almost at once. I did not like the look of them, and I liked it even less when I took them to the scene of the crime and they hit with their truncheon a youth who simply happened to be hanging around. They made me get into their jeep, where I sat in the middle of the back seat blocked in by police to left and right, and with a rifle slung over the seat in front of me. I was afraid again, as I remembered how this was the way people were taken away in the time of the dictatorship.

But a written police report is essential, for without that there can be no insurance claim and no replacing of documents such as my passport. In the police station the chief policeman took my statement, and was painfully slow on the uptake. I asked him to show me where we were on a wall map of the barrio. He did not know. What I had lost included an air ticket, a Psion palmtop computer, 4 credit cards, a cheque for $2,739 and three million guaraníes in cash (£461) – a fantastic taking in Paraguayan terms.

Of course I knew the usual advice for walking around Asunción – to carry the minimum of cash in case of robbery – but I had visited the bank that morning and the money included scholarships for poor students in Santa María. This is a cash economy, and even the university in San Ignacio looked puzzled at my suggestion that I might make payments directly by bank transfer.

But of all the things I lost, the worst was to lose all my phone numbers, for now I could not even ring my best friends in Santa María to get their support. It took nearly two more days before I could successfully make that contact.

As I paced up and down in the forecourt waiting for my release I said the *Anima Christi* over and over. '... Body of Christ, save me. Blood of Christ, inebriate me. Water from the side of Christ, wash me. Passion of Christ, strengthen me. O good Jesus, hear me. Within your wounds, hide me. Separated from you let me never be. From the malicious enemy, defend me. At the hour of my death call me ...' As I recited it, my tears began to be released, for it seemed to be written just for me – for someone who was frightened and vulnerable and whose memory and imagination was overflowing with blood and fear and death.

What happened to me is in no way unusual: both the friends I was staying with have suffered armed robberies in the street. I came here to Paraguay to share in the lives of the people with all the suffering that comes from poverty. Up till now I have seen that at close hand, yet always through a protective glass window. Now I have had a baptism into the reality of their lives, I cannot say I regret it.

(First published 20 April 2002.)

15

Why don't you telephone?

With rain pelting down, and thunder claps breaking directly overhead, my thoughts turn to the sorrows of Santa María. Tomorrow the heat will break through again, and those who have wept will laugh again, with that indestructible Latin American *alegría*. The struggle goes on: in the words of a famous hymn, *Hay que seguir andando no más*, 'We just have to keep going'.

Now after nearly two years here, I have a much more intimate knowledge of people's lives and how it hurts to be poor. Yet I still find myself caught out by my failure to anticipate problems. 'Why don't you telephone?' I said to a friend, who was turning his mobile phone over and over in his hand as he agonised over what to do in a moment of emergency. 'Because I have not got a phone card', he said. He can afford a £1.40 card once a month, and it lasts him about five minutes. Seriously.

I have got used to the fact that only one of the teachers learning English with me can afford to ring me when she cannot come to class, but I had not realised that the reason why another has only been coming a couple of times a week recently, instead of every day, is that she could not afford the petrol for her motorbike on the ten-minute run. People here hate asking for money just as much as you and I would. So she had said nothing, and it was only when I heard someone else commiserating with her about the severity of the economic crisis that I asked, and found out the truth.

So what does poverty mean here? I have seen some searing examples recently. Being poor means that when you are in love with a girl in another town, you cannot ring her, that you cannot visit her, that you cannot even write letters to her because you cannot afford a stamp. What can hurt more than that? Being poor means that when your partner beats you up and leaves you with bruises all down your body, you cannot escape with your children to the safety of your mother's house, because you cannot afford the £3 fare to get there. Being poor means that when your girlfriend becomes pregnant, and goes to live somewhere else in the country, you never know, even 20 years later, whether or not you have a child.

Being poor as a child means that you go to school without breakfast, and ask permission from your teacher to come home at break time, in the hope that your father has found something for you to eat. Being poor as a child means that you cry during your lessons from hunger.

Being poor means that when your newborn baby dies, and you are in the most critical moment of distress, you have not got the money for the coffin and have to go up and down the street begging from your neighbours, so you can bury the body within 48 hours before it goes rotten in the heat. (The law does not permit a burial without a coffin.) Being poor means that when you become accidentally pregnant, you do not go for antenatal checks, but you swallow the ignorant oral tradition your mother tells you about eating very little so that the baby will not grow big and give you a hard birth. Then in your weakened state and with an unskilled midwife you nearly die in childbirth from haemorrhaging, and your baby nearly dies too.

Being poor means that when you are sick with giardia from dirty water, and the doctor tells you to come back for a check-up in a month's time, you do not go because you could not afford the medicine and vitamins he prescribed, and you are ashamed to admit that you have not followed his instructions. So you wait until you are vomiting and listless and your intestines are crawling with great clumps of the worm, and then someone drives you to see the doctor again, and he gives you another prescription for the same medicine and vitamins to be taken over a much longer period, so that you are locked into a vicious circle of failure and worse illness.

Living among the poor means that when you ask in a shop for envelopes, you are handed one envelope, and when you ask for sticking plasters, you are handed one sticking plaster. When I received a request for some *ayuda* ('help') for the parish's youth event for Easter, it turned out I was being asked to donate 50 sheets of paper. 'Are you sure that is all you want?' I asked. 'Yes,' came the answer, 'because we can tear them in two and make them go round 100 people.' And when there were a few sheets over at the end, I was offered them back again.

I am living among people I love, and I live simply to share their lives as far as I can. But I cannot fool them, for they know perfectly well that I can tap resources on a scale that makes their mind boggle. The closer I come to seeing the inner face of my friends' poverty, the more I realise that however much I may try to live like them, the gap between us is a yawning chasm.

(*First published 25 May 2002.*)

16

Feast of San Juan

These are dark days in Santa María. Winter has set in with a vengeance
and the rains have made everything damp. My matches won't light and
my clothes won't dry. The electricity goes off for hours on end and then I
cannot work because my shutters are closed to keep the cold wind from
blowing through the paneless windows, and I haven't got light to see by.
When darkness falls the air turns so chill that it slices through my
thermal underwear and the only thing to do is fill a hot water bottle (if I
can light my matches and as long as the calor gas canister does not run
out) and go to bed.

On one of these bitter evenings, 24 June, I braved the weather and went
out to participate in the traditional feast of San Juan, which appropriately for the season is celebrated with fire. It is a typically Paraguayan
festival, with all the games carrying Guaraní names. The most popular
activity is the *pelota tatá*, the fireball, when a tightly bound ball of rags is
doused with petrol and set fire to; it is then kicked around with vigour,
into the heart of the screaming, dodging crowd. It is dangerous, but then
that is the thrill of it.

A similar game is the *toro kandil*, when men run under a fake bullskin
to charge the crowd with flaming horns. Then there is the *Judas kái*, when
a stuffed Judas figure – like a Guy Fawkes – is hung up high and burned,

with firecrackers exploding inside it in all directions. Most distasteful – and happily omitted on this occasion – is the *mbarakajá karrera*, a race between cats who have a burning cloth tied to their tails to make them run faster.

Those few of us who could afford to do so bought a measure of firewater and coke to pass around and warm our stomachs, and as the evening grew to a close we gathered around the dying bonfire for the climax. The burning embers were raked out to make a flat, red, fiery carpet, and those who were brave enough took off their shoes and socks and walked through the middle of it. At least four leisurely strides were needed, and it was done as calmly as walking from one side of a room to the other. 'Why doesn't it burn the feet?' I asked. I was told, 'Because tonight is the feast of San Juan, and he is the lord of the fire.'

It was a great night, but it ended tragically. A fight began as the last people left, and two young men were dragged away by three drunken youths, and robbed of their trainers, an anorak, their money and a mobile phone. Within a couple of weeks five youths had been arrested for the crime and locked up in the Abrahan-kué penitentiary, the same prison where some of my friends had been encarcerated during the Stroessner years. These days criminals usually get away scot-free because no one dares to denounce them for fear of becoming the next victim. So at first I was glad to hear that there had been arrests.

But my satisfaction turned to alarm when I heard that one was Carlos, a very pleasant young man who had danced with me with tireless energy on the night of my birthday party. Everyone was united in telling me he was innocent of this crime and was a good person who had never been involved in any such trouble. A couple of days later I cadged a lift with a friend and went to visit him in prison.

The penitentiary is deceptively informal. The padlock is undone on the gate and you can simply open it and walk into the grassy yard where the prisoners are sitting around, doing nothing. This is the outer part of the prison, where people pay for slightly better food and slightly less overcrowded cells (only ten to a room). Prisoners come through to here from the more dire interior when they have visits. No one wears uniform, and there are no activities apart from a twice daily roll call. 'Doing time' is a very appropriate phrase for a Paraguayan jail sentence.

Carlos came over to greet me with a very warm hug. He had been at the San Juan fiesta but had not been present at the fight, and had no idea of how his name came to be given to the police. He had nothing to read inside and was dying of boredom. He had been in Abrahan-kué already for six days and today was his birthday. I had not known that, and was glad I had brought him a bag of chocolates.

Carlos told me he had been to the tribunal that morning with his lawyer and was waiting for news of the judge's decision. While I was with him he received the happy news that he was to be released, and after another visit to the tribunal and more formalities back at the prison he walked through the gate to freedom at my side. 'You'll have to chalk it up to experience,' I said. Even the sun was smiling.

(*First published 3 August 2002.*)

17

Fiesta patronal

The *fiesta patronal* of Santa María was on 8 September, the birthday of the Virgin, and was celebrated in style. For the nine days beforehand there were nightly masses – packed out with people from the outlying *compañías,* followed by a bring-and-share supper, each night in a different home. On the last night, 7 September, we were in the house of Miriam, the teacher who was almost killed in a motorbike accident last year (see p.21). She still spends much of the day in bed, though she can now walk a few steps around her bedroom on her crutches; for the community supper she sat up in a wheelchair, proud that she had been able to prepare some of the food.

The next morning everyone gathered in front of the church at 8.30 am. This area is now looking quite attractive, with paving and flower beds and lamps, thanks to 'royalties' from the Itaipú dam. Itaipú (the 'noisy stone' in Guaraní) is on the River Paraná, on the border between Paraguay and Brazil, and was until recently the largest hydroelectric project in the world. It was begun in 1975, in the time of the corrupt Stroessner dictatorship, and the whole project was ringed with fraud from start to finish. Building firms would present inflated bills, which government officials would pay in return for their own cut of the extra money.

Things have not changed much. The bill that the local government of Santa María received for the paved area in front of the church was over one hundred million guaraníes (nearly £10,000). When a new Liberal mayor was voted in, shortly after the bill was paid, he thought it seemed rather a lot, so he ordered an audit of its true cost, against the will (I wonder why) of some of the Colorado members of the council who had authorised the works. The bill turned out to be almost double what it should have been, and the building firm had to repay the extra money, which was used to build a new slaughter house.

It was onto this new terrace that the magnificent statue of Santa María de Fe was carried out on 8 September – a great wooden carving some 300 years old, which normally stands high and tall on the wall behind the altar. The Virgin wears a silver, jewelled crown and a gold dress, and is standing on a crescent moon – in other words she is the 'woman clothed with the sun, with the moon under her feet, and on her head a crown of twelve stars' (*Revelation 12.1*). Her face is hauntingly beautiful and arresting in its gaze, and her carved black hair falls loosely down her back, zigzagging as though just released from a plait. She holds the infant high in her left arm, and he points up to her face, so that the attention is drawn from Jesus to Mary, and not the other way round. Of all the former Jesuit reductions in Paraguay – San Ignacio, Santa Rosa, San Cosme y Damián, Santiago, Trinidad and Jesús – Santa María surely has the most outstanding patronal statue.

Preceded by a line of bishop and clergy, and followed by a band and a multitude of people that crammed the wide red-earth roads, the procession made its slow way around town, before returning to the square for an open-air Mass celebrated by the fiery Bishop Mario Melanio Medina, who condemned the selfishness of the rich countries, in the light of the recent Johannesburg discussions, and emphasised the importance of Christian communities to give solidarity and strength to the people. Two animators from the communities – my friend Demetria and the carpenter Ladislao – then stepped forward with a display showing how the Christian communities formed a net of solidarity in the areas of health, education, economy, social organisation and celebration.

As the Virgin made her majestic way back into her church, a display of folklore began. Four girls did a folk dance with jugs, another girl stepped forward and read a Guaraní poem she had written to *Tupãsý* (the mother of God), and another danced balancing a bottle on her head. Then there was a buffet lunch in the garden of the retreat house.

The celebrations went on all day. On a stretch of track at the edge of the village there were competitions on horseback, with young men from the *compañías* wearing the typical dress of Paraguayan cowboys: boots, dark-blue baggy breeches, striped cummerbunds, light-blue or checked shirts, with a white handkerchief tied round the neck and a wide-brimmed *sombrero* on the head. They rode with long reins, leaning backwards, with their legs sticking forward and long in the stirrup – quite the opposite style from Europe. A high T-shaped structure on the track had two tiny rings hung from it, with a red ribbon marking each for visibility. The game was to gallop under the T and spear the ring with a little twig held in the hand. It was very difficult indeed, and few managed to bear away the ring and receive a prize.

The second competition was jumping, and I was amazed that neither horses nor riders seemed to have the remotest idea of how to get over a jump. The technique was to gallop at the bar as fast as possible in the hope that the horse would not shy. It was an exceedingly ineffective method: some horses charged straight through the bar and some ran round the side, while those that did attempt to jump took off too late and knocked the bar off with their front knees. But it made good entertainment.

(*First published 28 September 2002.*)

50

18

You can't bank on anything

'You should get yourself a revolver', my neighbour Ismael told me. Everyone in Santa María is talking about Saturday night's break-in to the house of Lucila, who teaches special-needs pupils at the school (like my friend, Nilsa, a deaf-and-dumb girl). 'These things never used to happen in Santa María,' said Ismael. 'It's something new with the growing poverty, and everyone is afraid.'

For some months now there have been regular thefts of chickens from the gardens of the poor, and killings of cattle by night, because the meat can be sold. But a new run of robberies began with a break-in to the streetstall right plumb in front of the 24-hour-manned police station. If the police are not paid a cut to keep quiet, it can be the police themselves who carry out the robberies, or so I was told by Lucila's aunt Felipa, when I went this morning to fetch my milk fresh from her cow. If people cannot trust the police to protect them, what else can they do but think in terms of revolvers?

Whoever burgled Lucila's house knew that she had a new Philips television with a large screen. (Like everything else in Paraguay, it was bought on hire purchase, which leaves Lucila a big bill to pay for no television.) And they knew that she was safely out of Santa María at a birthday party in the *compañía* of San Juan Berchmans. They struck between midnight and 1.00 am by a somewhat biblical method of gaining entry – taking the tiles off the roof and dropping in from above.

They took not only the television and the video (as they would also in England) but also her new shoes, some boots, her daughter's school uniform, some anoraks, an eiderdown, sheets from the beds, and a host of other items that no European thief would think worth bothering about but are all worth something here.

Teachers are not paid a lot but in Santa María they are the better off, even though their state income is not as secure as it used to be. In both September and October they had to go on strike before the government would pay them their monthly salary. Since Paraguay took out a 90 million dollar loan in June to help counter a huge decrease in the value of the guaraní, the IMF has demanded a bundle of new austerity measures. Failure to pay salaries is not supposed to be one of them, but when government ministers have their hand in the till, the money has to come from somewhere.

The police and the government are not the only institutions that people mistrust. They mistrust the banks too. Paraguay is a cash economy, which I find a constant cause of bewilderment. When our Institute for the poor bought some expensive laboratory equipment for its food technology classes, I went to great trouble to get the money in a banker's draft so it would be safe. But no sooner had the company director got the cheque in his hand than he changed it straight back into 'real money'.

Real money means torn, dirty notes with broken edges and cracks down the middle. The lower denominations become so drenched in Paraguayan sweat that you can smell their rank odour even as you take them in your hands. Any other country would divide their currency by 1,000 so that the smallest note was for one guaraní, not a thousand guaraníes (10 pence). But Paraguay cannot afford to replace the notes.

I had the same experience over a cheque for Miriam, the schoolteacher who had the motor-bike accident. I went to great trouble to get the money to open the account in the form of a cheque and together we had an interview with the bank manager. 'Why did you bring the money like this?' he said, fingering the nice, clean, new cheque with suspicion, as though he had never seen one before. 'Can you go back to Asunción to change it?'

A similar conversation took place when I went to speak with Dante and his wife Fátima over the purchase of a building for the Institute. 'Would you mind letting us have the money split into two cheques rather than one?' they asked. 'It will be safer that way.' I explained that the money would be safe anyway because if the cheque was stolen it would be stopped and re-issued. (This is exactly what had happened when I had a cheque for $2,737 stolen, see p.40.) That was not the problem, they said. If there were two cheques they could cash them one at a time and only lose half the money if they were robbed.

I was mystified. 'But surely you don't think the money will be safer in cash in your house than it would be in the bank?' I asked. 'Here in Paraguay,' they said, 'we cannot trust the banks.' I knew that one of the two banks in San Ignacio was the state-run Banco Nacional de Fomento and had a reputation for stealing its customers' money, but the other bank was a private bank and should be reliable.

All the same, I had to admit that my own bank, the Banco Alemán, had gone bust in June in the fall-out of the Argentinian economic collapse, despite being considered one of the two most secure banks in the country. I had lost money. 'There you are,' said Dante and Fátima triumphantly, 'you cannot trust a bank.' They had seen a whole domino effect of collapsing banks only a few years before I had come to Paraguay.

And if you cannot trust a bank, and cannot trust a state salary, and cannot trust the police, then what can you trust? Surely not a revolver?

(*First published 26 October 2002.*)

19

The pig

I was startled yesterday to hear a frantic, terrified shrieking from next door. I ran out into the garden, and there were four men with a knife. 'They are going to kill the pig,' said Luis, my gardener. With Christmas upon us this is the start of the pig-killing season. I have often asked to see the killing of a pig and never arrived in time. This time I saw it all. 'When we killed our pig, we did it with only three of us,' boasted Luis.

Paraguayan pigs are greyish black rather than pink, and have straight rather than curly tails. They have big ugly snouts and neat, small bottoms. They live in people's back gardens and gobble up the scraps and love sitting in mud. Sometimes they are confined in pig sties and sometimes they are just tied up. When they get loose they can run surprisingly fast.

This pig was past running. One man was holding its back legs, tied together with a rope, another its front legs, also secured with a rope, and another its head. All three were exercising their full weight to hold the agonised animal still on the ground. Ismael was applying the knife to the throat, making a small hole through which the blood drained slowly into a dish and was regularly tipped out into a bucket. Nothing is wasted.

It was only when the pig felt the knife in its throat that it began to scream, and it went on screaming for quite a long time, until its life force had poured out and the legs went lifeless. Then it was lifted onto a bench, and jugs of boiling water were straightaway poured over the black outer skin, which was scraped off with spoons and knives like a thin paper, leaving a white membrane beneath. If this is not done at once, the skin will not peel off.

The next step was to hang the pig up from a beam and cut out the intestines, which would be thrown on a dump and eaten by dogs. The trotters were discarded, and the body was cut into six big slabs of meat: four legs and two sides.

I presumed that Ismael was killing his own pig, but was amazed afterwards to see his animal looking perfectly happy and calm and chomping away, despite having witnessed the slaughter and heard the terrible screams. It must be really stupid if it does not realise it is awaiting the same fate.

The pig in question was bought that morning for 120,000 guaraníes (£12). 'It's cheaper to kill one yourself,' explained Ismael. 'Besides which, you can see what sort of animal you are getting – whether it is a nice domestic pig that has fed on family leftovers, or only a pig from the fields that has had nothing but grass and is less fatty: it will taste more like beef.'

'How much would you pay for the meat if you did not kill the pig yourself?' I asked. 'Oh, at least 125,000', said Ismael. All that work to save 50 pence? 'Well you get all the extras as well,' said Ismael, 'the head, the innards …'

The next day we ate these extras, and they invited me to share them. 'It's not every day you kill a pig,' they said, 'it's a very special treat.' I have seen paintings of boars' heads in medieval banquets, but never actually eaten one before. It had been boiled for five hours, having only had removed the tip of its nose and the inner complexities of its ears, and the flesh was brown and shrunk off the skull, revealing its full set of teeth and two little tusks, which were later removed for putting on keyrings.

The jaws were wrenched apart to get at the tongue, and the eye hung out, a white shrunken blob in a brown shrunken blob. 'Who is going to eat that?' I asked, 'I'm not.' 'Aren't you?' said Ismael, 'Do share it with me. Don't you know that crows regard the eyes as such a delicacy that they will pluck them out of animals even before they are dead?'

This pig was four or five years old and I asked why it was so old. 'Because it was used for breeding,' Ismael said. 'Later it was castrated, and then sold for eating.'

'Why was it castrated?' I asked.

'Because you could not eat it otherwise: the males smell awful. You have to castrate them at least three months before you want to eat them.'

'Did you do the castrating?' I asked.

'Not on this one, but I've done it on others.'

'I bet they scream then as well.'

'You bet they do.'

The head was not the only 'extra' on the table. There was also a plate of neck pieces, and a big bowl piled high with red blood and gore and the chopped heart, kidney and liver – the ingredients of blood pudding without even the cosmetics of the sausage cover.

'It's delicious, isn't it?' they kept on saying, 'Do you like it? Do you like it?'

I took small portions and played the simple foreigner: 'I have to get used to it,' I said. 'This is the first time I've eaten a pig's head.' And I realised I must have seemed in my own way as naive and ignorant – but hardly as appreciative – as the *campesina* I took to Asunción's tiny airport, who said it was one of the greatest experiences of her life to go up and down an escalator.

(*Never before published; written 8 December 2002.*)

20

The crib

One night when I was in the retreat house I borrowed the key to the museum of Santa María and crept in alone when it was dark. I wanted to pay a night visit to the remarkable, large crib that is one of the most famous art works to survive from the Jesuit-Guaraní period.

The building is one of the original houses from the reduction, and is itself somewhat reminiscent of the barn of the nativity, with its stone walls 90 centimetres thick, and its line of dark rooms without windows. To get to the crib you must pass through four rooms of saints and angels, all dramatically carved, with robes flowing as though whipped by the wind, and faces alive with emotion. I remembered how Ignatius tells us to place ourselves in prayer 'before the angels and saints who intercede for me', and as I looked up at the statues in the silence of the night, turning my gaze from face to face, each one seemed to have its lips parted as though it was singing in honour of the Christ child, 'Glory to God'.

In the fifth room I reached the group of the nativity, which is displayed at eye level. There is no ox and no ass – and there has never been a custom in Paraguay of including an ox at the crib. But there are five sheep, a black long-snouted peccary, a tinamou bird, three shepherds, three magi, a Joseph, a big Mary seated on a chair, and a baby lying on a cushion. The original baby was stolen from the museum some years ago, and in its place lies a baby borrowed from another group, but he makes a very convincing substitute.

The most dominating figure is Mary – one of the most expressive of many Marys in our museum, even though browned by age. From her size alone it is evident that she did not originally come from this group, and it is probable that she is a Mary of the Annunciation. Her face has the look of a girl in the presence of her admiring lover, both vulnerable and honoured, flushed with incredulous joy.

Seated on a simple chair she looks downwards, with a book clasped in one hand and her other hand to her breast as though at the moment of replying to Gabriel, 'Let it be done unto me.' In English it sounds longwinded and clumsy, but in Latin, Spanish and Guaraní this fundamental prayerful attitude of open acceptance is captured in a single word: *fiat ... hágase ... tojejapo.* It has become a universal prayer of Christians, expressing a joyful and humble response towards God.

One of the shepherds touches me greatly, because he is a little disabled man with a slight hunchback and one leg longer than the other, so that he limps. So lifelike is this figure, and so unusual is the conception, that I imagine he was a real member of the Christian community who was immortalised by the artist on account of his devotion. Unlike his chatty neighbour, his mouth is not open to speak, but he just walks in towards Jesus, limpingly, silently, faithfully. With one arm he holds a lamb, which he brings as a gift, and the other arm is stretched out in self-offering. He is a role model for poor workers of the field – *campesinos* today, and Guaraní indigenous in the time of the reduction.

The first of the magi is a fair-haired man with long hair and an open mouth, who seems to be speaking with animation, gesturing with the finger and thumb of his right hand as if to say, 'It was just so'. Secondly there is a black-skinned man of a quite different build: erect and dignified he too has his hand outstretched as if recounting the events of the journey, but his manner is more tranquil. And thirdly there is a man on his knees with his arms crossed humbly across his breast: he has no words, but he is lost in utter, engrossed admiration of the child before his eyes.

The meaning of the journey of the magi for our age is that Europeans should go in pilgrimage not just west, but south-west, and learn their faith from the poor of the *campo*. They may be hidden from the eyes of the world, but they live a God-filled life in harmony with nature, sur-rounded by animals. The magi meant well, and the European evangelis-ers meant well, but sadly in their wake they brought death – the magi through the information they gave to Herod, that led to the slaughter of the innocents; the Europeans through the introduction of hitherto unknown illnesses, that also led to deaths on a terrifying scale. Would the people of the Americas have been better off if the Europeans had never come? It is hard to answer that.

In one sense, of course they would have been: they would not have suffered the near genocide of tribes who were enslaved, driven off their land, and decimated by hard labour and disease. And yet at the same time they wanted to reach out to the white settlers, to welcome them and learn from them skills they would never have reached on their own – reading and writing, skills in construction and music and art. Today they want to learn the use of the computer and the internet, to transport their goods on asphalted roads and to cure illnesses with antiobiotics.

So once again the 'wise' who come with respect are welcomed, as Mary welcomed the magi. And once again the 'wise' must become disciples, and learn from the little ones of this world.

(*Edited from an article first published 21/28 December 2002.*)

CRCR   SOSO

Visiting the Santa María museum at night is no longer possible because there is an alarm.

21

Crocodile and harp music

You know things are really bad when you see branches of McDonald's close down. Five branches of the great symbol of US-driven globalisation have now shut. Paraguayans love their hamburgers, but they just do not have money to buy them any more. There is not money for anything.

In Santa María I have seen a fax shop open, and close again. A computer school open, and close again. A photocopying shop open, and close again. A bakery open, and close again. And a branch of a credit union open, and close again.

The supermarkets are closing too: the María Cristina chain has closed three of its five branches, and Stock – one of the biggest chains – has shut a shop too. It is hard for a European to come to terms with a world in which supermarkets retract rather than expand, but such is the world of the South American recession since the crisis in Mercosur (the South American common market) began to bite. Last year the Argentinian peso lost 251 per cent of its value against the dollar, the Uruguayan peso lost 93 per cent, the Brazilian real lost 52 per cent, and the Paraguayan guaraní lost 46 per cent.

There was a new blow yesterday. When I went to San Ignacio to draw out money, I found workmen taking down the big green sign above the Banco Continental, which has the only cash machine for miles around. I assumed it was a facelift, until the workmen told me there was no point in me going inside. It was all over. You mean? Yes. For this town at least. Caput. Curtains. I gaped in disbelief. How was I going to be able to draw out money in the future, to feed the constant run of little projects I am supporting, all of which have to be paid in cash? But it stands to reason, if there is no money circulating there will be no business for the banks either.

According to economic logic, as the currency loses its value, Paraguayan products will become more competitive and sell better, and cheaper labour costs will encourage foreign investors to build factories here. It never happens, not one little bit. No one wants to do business in Paraguay, because they do not trust the communications, or the quality control, or the accounting.

The President of the Republic, Luis González Macchi, is now facing impeachment for his incompetence and corruption in running the country. There is no new exposure, but the time has only recently become ripe for making a gesture of protest. There is a presidential election coming up on 27 April, and if the ruling Colorado party can distance itself at the last moment from the current President it stands a better chance of being re-elected.

Railing against the government may let off some frustration, but what is the solution? I believe there are two avenues to be pursued. One is to grow more food. Working the land is not very fashionable – more young people want to study computing – and with agriculture at the pre-industrial-revolution stage, we are talking about back-breaking work in the heat of the sun to achieve nothing more than subsistence. But self-sufficient subsistence is far better than indebtedness and hunger.

As my own tiny contribution to this, I have turned over my back garden to two poor families, which also happens to solve my gardening problems. As an Englishwoman I liked the romantically long meadow grass, dotted with wild flowers, that I had before, but my neighbours complained that it provided a shady spot for poisonous snakes to flourish. I was urged to use weedkiller, which is regarded as quick and modern. But I resisted, after consulting a couple of agriculturalists who confirmed that it would 'set a bad example'.

Instead I had a yoke of oxen brought in to plough up the weeds. Negro, who drove them, was a cheerful chap, lithe and energetic with a baggy white shirt and a big *sombrero*. He had no shoes, because he is so poor, and padded barefoot round the ground shouting out the respective names of the oxen to steer them. He was very amused that I wanted to take photos. After the ploughing, a big rake was attached to the yoke to drag up the dug-out grass. In a day the oxen had achieved as much as a man would in a fortnight. And two families have now accepted the invitation to sow beans there, on the understanding that they keep the ground clear of weeds organically.

The other solution to Paraguay's economic crisis, I believe, is to increase exports. I have seen a little appliqué bag, sold by our craft workshop here in Paraguay for 13,000 guaraníes (less than two dollars), re-sold in the United States for $12.50. By slowly building up a small-scale mail-order service, with use of email, our women can earn the foreign retail price directly with minimal deductions. And as the dollar rises so too will their income.

Despite all the problems, let no one think that life is all bad here. At New Year I feasted on freshly caught crocodile and sat outside the house of the local carpenter listening to live harp music before the setting sun. 'This is the good life,' I thought. Paraguay's biggest untapped resource for earning foreign currency could prove to be tourism for adventurous and discerning travellers, in this undiscovered and dirt-cheap land.

(*First published 1 February 2003.*)

ରାର   ဿၜ

Santa María craft products can now be seen on the website www.santamariadefe.com *and ordered by email to* info@santamariadefe.com.

I later discovered that serving crocodile meat is illegal in Paraguay: it is a law more honoured in the breach than the observance in private homes, but it does prevent crocodile being served in restaurants.

Things are improving in Paraguay, and foreign investment is now slowly beginning.

22

Room of the Passion

At Christmastime I wrote about the crib in the museum of Santa María. But the most remarkable works from the period of the old Jesuit missions are statues of the Passion: the museum has a whole room devoted to them. This year a Cuban Jesuit, Carlos de la Cruz, who had been parish priest here, came back to Santa María to make a radio programme with me for Good Friday, based on these works of art and on the life of the local people (*BBC Radio 4, 18 April 3.00 pm*).

The statues from the time of the reduction are life-size, or nearly life-size, carved in wood and painted. All are drenched in Ignatian spirituality, with its potent combination of the sensual and the contemplative. Some, known by the Guaraní name of *Tupãsý Ñuvaitĩ* ('the encounter of the Mother of God'), portray the resurrection appearance of Christ to his mother – a meditation which appears in Ignatius' *Spiritual Exercises,* though not in scripture. These statues of the wondering Mary, her hands stretching forward in joy, and their accompanying statues of Christ risen from the grave, formed the focus of a dawn procession on Easter Sunday.

The museum is a long building, original to the reduction, with a portico running the full length – impressive and very solid, with light entering through its big doors rather than through windows. Most of the rooms now have interconnecting doors inside, though originally they were separate family units, but to enter the final room – the Room of the Passion – you have to go outside again to the portico, and unlock a big, creaky door. Knowing how powerful are the images inside, I always find this entry a solemn one, like going into the sanctuary of a church.

The first person to open the museum to me had been Carlos de la Cruz in 1996, on the day I fell in love with Santa María. And now I was stepping with him again into the Room of the Passion, as though into the wounded heart of this small town that we both love so dearly – a town with its own history of pain.

Going clockwise around the room is the whole story of the Passion, beginning with an appealing and rather childlike figure of Jesus on a donkey, which is brought out to be carried in procession during the Palm Sunday liturgy. After that comes a large and powerful statue of Jesus on his knees praying, called 'Christ in the Garden'. While most of the statues were carved by the indigenous, this one is said to have been carved by the great Jesuit from the Tyrol, Anton Sepp (1691–1767), musician and polymath, when he tended the people of Santa María through a plague of smallpox. Jesus has his arms outstretched and his palms lifted, simultaneously pleading and offering himself – no doubt just what Sepp was feeling as he tended the sick, 20 or 30 of whom were dying each day.

Next is a distinctive and smaller figure, with an unusual theme: it is Peter weeping. One hand points up, and his head tilts back, as though he is saying, 'Hush there! Do you hear it?' And as he listens to the cock crow, the painted tears plunge down his cheeks. He is not crumpled by his sin, because he knows he is loved, but the grief flows through him as he realizes what he has done and how he can never put the clock back again.

A group of three statues comes next, all portraying the same scene: Jesus scourged at the pillar. While all three are powerful, the central figure is perhaps the most moving. This is a small and very indigenous Jesus, dark and humble, silent as a sheep before its slaughterers. He is cut all over his body and spattered with blood, and on his left cheek is a wound in the shape of a red crescent moon, with three drops of blood falling from it – a distinctive and decorative mark reminiscent of native face-painting. He looks straight ahead, intent and silent, the representative of all the voiceless indigenous peoples of the world who have suffered injustice, slavery and slaughter, just as the Guaraní of this area were decimated at the hands of the Portuguese *bandeirantes*. This Jesus is clearly battered physically, but it is his mental hurt that is so eloquent. He says nothing, but he looks at you, and you are filled with shame. He has been betrayed by his friend, and you are the friend who betrayed him.

After this group comes Christ carrying his cross – though this damaged figure is now without its cross – and then Christ crucified, his forehead furrowed by pain, and the Beloved Disciple and the Virgin of Sorrows at his feet. Another statue from the other half of the museum should really belong in this room – Mary with her hands joined in prayer, her eyes slightly raised and her face drained and anguished. She is surely contemplating her son on the cross. Her concentration is haunting, and as you look into her eyes you find there a gaze so steady and so other-absorbed that you can almost see the cross mirrored in her pupils.

The next figure is called the *Cristo Yacente*, which means 'Christ lying down'. It is an 'articulated' figure, that is, its arms are hinged at the shoulders, so that they can be lifted up in a crucified posture, or folded down for entombment. What is most remarkable is the face – quite different both from the figure at the pillar and the figure on the cross. This Christ is noble and intelligent and at peace – his brow smooth, and his eyes not so much reproaching as engaging the observer in a deep soul-to-soul exploration. Christ lies dead, his face and body black and red, bruised and blooded; yet in his eyes we already see the victory.

As Carlos meditated on the Passion with me, standing before these figures of pain, he remembered the brutal persecution that he had known, under the dictatorship of General Stroessner (1954–89). Some of the earliest Christian base communities, the *Ligas Agrarias Cristianas*, had been formed in this area during the dictatorship, and they were bloodily wiped out. The *Pascua Dolorosa* (the 'Sorrowful Easter') of 1976 marked the high point of the repression, when a number of local people were arrested, tortured, and imprisoned, 'for no other crime than trying to be authentic Christians – to live by the Word of the Lord, live in community, and live in solidarity among themselves,' said Carlos.

Carlos quietly remembered one case: 'A man was taken from his house, from in front of his wife and his children, and he was taken to the public square, where he was tied to a tree. There he was tortured in the public eye. Everyone could see it happening, and nobody did anything. They did not kill him, they just let him die slowly, slowly, and nobody came to help him. And I know the family right now,' added Carlos, 'and I know that they still keep the faith.'

As we complete the circle of the room we come to the *feretro* (the bier), designed for procession on Good Friday. And high on the wall above the *feretro* are angel heads, with tears streaming from their eyes.

(*First published 19 April 2003.*)

ଔଔ   ဢဢ

The custom of the Tupāsý Ñuvaitī procession was restored in Santa María in 2006.

23

Oral culture

Rural Paraguay is an oral culture, not a written culture. What does that mean?

It means that many of the familiar handholds are not there, in a way that never ceases to surprise me.

When someone comes to visit me and I am out, they never think of leaving a note. When I am expecting someone to visit me and I have to go out, I leave a message, taped prominently to the door, but they do not think of looking at it. Oh yes, they said, they saw a piece of paper there, but they never thought it might be a note for them.

When someone has something to buy or to sell – a car, a house, a bicycle – they ask around. There is no system of classified ads, not even for jobs. Teaching jobs have to be publicly advertised, but there is nowhere to place the ad. It means that you have to travel the country and ask in person at the office in each region.

When there is a local event – a bullfight, a meeting, a festival – there is no written announcement. There is no local newspaper, no parish news-letter, no town noticeboard, where it can be advertised. The only effective way local news gets around is by what they call *radio so'o*, which means (in Guaraní) 'the radio of the flesh'. Even when I put an announcement on the local radio, the people lose the piece of paper I have written it on and repeat an approximation from memory.

On the rare occasions when a leaflet is produced then the written information is likely to be wrong. At the Santiago *Fiesta de la Tradición Misionera*, none of the four events advertised for the Friday morning happened, and no one turned up for them. On Sunday morning only one event was advertised, and thousands turned up. People knew what was going to happen, not from the leaflet but from word of mouth.

No one gives birthday cards, or Christmas cards, or condolence cards. In church there are no hymn books, nor any mass sheets. People sing from memory, or they do not sing. When I write down the address of a customer on an order of craftwork, the women do not know that I have given them the address, because they do not know how to recognise an address. They do not know that you write it in separate lines, with a comma separating each, beginning with the smallest place and ending with the biggest.

Until the educational reform of the mid-nineties, no one was taught to read and write in their first language, Guaraní, until they were in second-ary school. The result is curious. When I go to a day event for the Christian communities, the discussion in little groups is in Guaraní, but one of the *campesinos* takes notes in Spanish. Then we meet again in plenary session and the secretary of the group reads back the notes fluently and without hesitation – not in Spanish but in Guaraní.

Written Spanish is full of errors, even from pupils who have passed through tertiary education. Accents are omitted or misplaced, 'b's and 'v's alternate without reason, as do 'c's and 's's, or 'm's and 'n's. People even spell their names in unusual ways without realising it: Alva, and Gricelda, and Mirian. Punctuation consists of occasional commas with hardly a full stop in sight, let alone a question mark or inverted commas. When I ask people why they do not put the punctuation in, they say they forget.

No one reads books. There is a free lending library here in Santa María, but no one uses it. People have plenty of time, but they spend it sitting in groups chatting and passing round the drink of *tereré*. Or if they are alone, they simply sit. The only Paraguayan I have observed regularly reading a book is the lavatory attendant on the first floor of the Super-centro shopping centre in Asunción. She sits there and reads all day long. Here in Paraguay where jobs are hard to come by, being a lavatory attendant is not necessarily a sign of poor education.

Due to the lack of written communication, when the national Post Office issued a set of Christmas stamps featuring the crib of Santa María, no one in Santa María knew about it, not even the post mistress (for she does not sell stamps, for no one writes letters). I found out about it by chance when I went to the post office in Asunción. Here is what the tourist leaflet – in Spanish and English – had to say about the Virgin on the new stamps:

'She is the dominant figure in this work, but not to remove the possibility of contemplate and adore the "Verbum", on the contrary, all in it, since the movements of her body and the costume to the fact of be sitting, with the head lean seeing her Son, the hands position, all the details drive us joint with shepherdess, the kings, the animals to walk to the centre, there where is the life; to acknowledge in that Child (in this "dollop of blood and meat") the scandalous Happening (scandalous yesterday, as today), the Presence of the Mystery in the world.'

But then, leaflets are for looking pretty, not for reading.

(*First published 28 June 2003.*)

24

A party every day

Santa María has been living through a week of intense festivities. On the first Saturday there was a confirmation, and the event was celebrated with the launch of the 'Santa María cavalry'. A procession of riders carrying flags came down my street and passed under a gateway of balloons and into a field to engage in horseback games. There was the usual sale of meat roasted on stakes, and plenty of loud music.

Our new local cavalry looked magnificent, and my 14-year-old neighbour María was very elegant on her uncle's horse, in the traditional dark-blue breeches, long black boots, white shirt, red neckerchief, colourful woven cummerbund and cowboy hat. No one ever wears a hard hat on a horse, and when two horses collided and a rider was left painfully writhing on the grass I was quite expecting a serious accident. Fortunately it turned out nothing worse than cuts and bruises.

On Thursday there was the official opening of the asphalt road that links us with the main Asunción–Encarnación highway. We have watched the stop – start construction of this for over two years, as the money originally allocated was stolen by the corrupt governor, and replacement funds came in dribs and drabs. The asphalting was proudly begun, first at one end, and after a long delay at the other end, until the money ran out again. For a while there was the total illusion of a proper road disappearing into the distance whether you looked from the Santa María end or from the turn-off from Ruta Uno. It was only if you actually tried to travel on it that you found you were shaken to pieces on all the bumpy stones in the middle bit.

The finished road today is hardly impressive. It is bumpy and pitted with holes, as barely a centimetre of asphalt covers the cobbles beneath. But it is smoother than what we had before, and we are now hoping that the bus companies will lower their fares. Many people simply cannot afford the 40 pence fare for the 40-minute journey to San Ignacio, and fewer bumps mean less wear and tear on vehicles. No longer will I sit and watch the screws in the floor shaking themselves loose before my very eyes.

The opening of the road was celebrated by what is known as a *caravana*: every bus, car and motorbike turned up to join in the jolly tooting procession, barely an hour or two after the last metre of asphalt was laid. Then we went into the church for speeches, and ended with a barbecue at the police station, with special guests invited to a huge sit-down dinner for 150 people. The dinner was Paraguayan-style: more roast meat than you can possibly consume ('that bit is cold, have another, try this different cut, this piece is more tender', etc.), piles of boiled *mandioca*, cold rice salad with a sliver of tomato, and no dessert.

On Friday our new president, Nicanor Duarte Frutos, elected on 27 April, 'assumed' the presidency. This assumption of power, always takes place on the feast of the Virgin Mary's Assumption, the same day as our capital city was founded. I do not have television, so I went round to Demetria's and glued myself to the box for this one day in the year. Politically it was enthralling, as an array of Latin American presidents arrived one by one, and were welcomed, seated in the front row, cheered (in some cases) and addressed by Nicanor. The loudest cheers were for Hugo Chávez of Venezuela and especially Fidel Castro of Cuba. The two are great pals.

There was a fascinating inverse relation between the amount of security each president had, and the degree of relaxation he exhumed. Chávez was very jolly, and no one could have guessed how precarious his position is within his country. Castro is a grand old man, dignified and heroic after surviving decades of resisting the mighty beast. Cuba is a friend of Paraguay, because of the medical help they give us. In Santa María we have a Cuban doctor on a two-year placement, and three of our local students are on scholarships to study medicine in Cuba. Another friend of Paraguay is Taiwan (or 'China', as it was called on the television commentary), which paid for our new parliament building, finished just in time for Nicanor's inauguration. Does that make Paraguay 'pro-communist' or 'anti-communist'? No one knows and no one cares.

On the following day was the 'ordination of the Sisters', as it is referred to locally – that is, their vows. Three Sisters of the Company of Mary Our Lady made their first vows, after spending a couple of years in the novitiate. They are beautiful and intelligent young women – two from poor families in the locality and one a trained vet from Asunción, who has had to work hard to get her Guaraní up to rural standards. Ada, one of the local girls, acted as spokesperson as she took the microphone and with eyes aglow with happiness told the packed church how they would accompany the life of the Christian communities, cost what it may.

The Sisters know and love the local people and their life here is a model of evangelical poverty – with no fridge, no television, no indoor running water, no flushing toilet, no heating, no glass in the windows, and no car. Yet they have made their little home – with its climbing creepers, blue check curtains, and large hospitable table – the prettiest house in the village. The kiss of peace was kept to the end of Mass, and never has there been such a swirl of people engaged in long and enthusiastic hugs. And if one day these Sisters were really to be ordained, it would seem to our *campesinos* the most natural thing in the world.

(*First published 30 August 2003.*)

ᦉᦉ ᦉᦉ

The Sisters' house now has a fridge, indoor running water and a flushing toilet, but still no television, heating or glass in the windows. And they now have a jeep.

25

A weight on my heart

Who is my neighbour? In the new year I was asked if I could help a mother whose son had cancer and who was selling all she had to pay for his treatment. I said I could not. On Tuesday he died, at four o'clock in the afternoon. 'Didn't you hear the crying at four?' the Sisters asked me. 'You could hear it from our house. The mother is just inconsolable.' Victor José had just turned 19.

The body was buried according to local custom 24 hours after the death. The least I could do was to go to the funeral, but I wondered what the mother would think of me. I must have been the only person who could possibly have saved him, and I had said 'No'. I do not think she saw me through her tears, and she made a prayer which went on and on, getting more and more desperate. The lay animator gently interrupted her and began the next hymn, providing a firm hand when the service could have dissolved into chaos.

Funerals are regularly led by laity here. The priest is not in Santa María every day and in a hot country a burial will not wait. By a tragic irony, this lay animator had heard that same morning that she had narrowly escaped a similar death sentence herself. A nurse had told her a week ago that she had cancer but now the test results showed that what she had was benign. She shared the good news with me, and then went on to the church to lead the liturgy for this young man who had not been so lucky.

I was standing in church next to a humble little woman who always makes a point of giving me the kiss of peace at Mass, and she sensed my upset and put her arm round me. I clung to her embrace, needing friends at a moment when I was lost in a mixture of doubt and guilt. Too late, too late, forever now too late. But could he have been saved?

I remembered keenly the mother's visit. An intermediary had asked if I would see her. I said I would, so long as she was told in advance that I could not help financially. When I heard it was cancer I had assumed it was a hopeless case, and the treatment offered was chemotherapy, which I supposed would do nothing more than buy him a little time.

I was impressed with Pabla when she came in the quiet heat of a summer night. She was a tall, gentle, intelligent woman, not originally one of the very poorest of Santa María, but now entering with dignity and peace her new life of impoverishment. I shared with her my suspicions that the chemotherapy would do nothing more than delay the day, and that if she went on selling all that she had she might lose both her son and her livelihood. She said, 'But the doctor told me that it was curable.'

When she had gone I rang a friend who is a doctor in Asunción and told her the diagnosis and the name of the doctor dealing with the case. She too thought it sounded bleak but said she would ring and make discreet professional enquiries. The reply was that Victor José had responded very well to the treatment. This ambiguous answer was the nearest I got to knowing if he could be saved.

After that doubt was sown in my mind I still did nothing. Or rather, I was busy doing a thousand other things. No one asked me for money a second time, and no one told me that, with all funds exhausted, he had come back to his home town to die. I heard nothing more until I heard with some shock that he was dead. No one has blamed me and no one will blame me, but should I blame myself?

Would I do, or fail to do, the same again? I probably would. I have all my reasons pat, but in the face of the possibly needless death of a young man they sound hollow excuses. I do not have a fund for health, only for education. I do not have time to administer a fund for health as well. Even when I am given money to spend at my discretion I could not spend on one individual without hundreds of similar cases turning up at my gate. I have to prioritise clearly achievable goals over narrow chances. In any case I did not come here to attempt the impossible task of solving all the problems of Santa María but rather to write a book, which is progressing all too slowly due to the demands on my time of aid work.

At the cemetery the custom is to open the coffin to give the relatives one last sight of their loved one. The family clustered tightly round but I slipped in as close as I could get and got a quick glimpse as the heads moved. It was enough to see how extraordinarily good-looking Victor José had been. Then the lid was nailed down again, the coffin was slipped into the slot of the grave, the mourners chucked in handfuls of earth, and the bricklayer rapidly and with awful finality ensured that he was gone for ever.

(*First published 27 September 2003.*)

ଓଋ   ৪০৪০

I have never yet found the time to write that book, and this collection of Tablet *pieces, which will do instead, has taken 11 years to see the light.*

26

Santa María craft

Turning travail into joy and the ugly into something beautiful: this is what our faith is about. The pain of the world brought us the goodness of the child in the crib. In the famous words of the *Exultet*: 'O necessary sin of Adam, to gain for us so great a Redeemer!' And in their own small way the women of Santa María are sharing in that miracle of transformation. The dust and tears, the sweat and hurt of life at its harshest are taken up by their needles and thread and embroidered into cloth pictures, that shine with colour, simplicity and hope.

The principal theme of the 30 women who form the sewing cooperative is the labour of the earth – for much of Paraguayan land is still worked with forks and hoes, and at best an ox cart. 'In toil shall you eat of the ground all the days of your life; thorns and thistles it shall bring forth for you … By the sweat of your face you shall eat bread, until you return to the ground' (*Genesis 3.17–19*).

An agricultural labourer will earn a pound for a day's sweat in the sun. When Negro came to plough up my back garden with a yoke of oxen, I asked him why he went barefoot. 'I would like to have shoes,' he said, 'but it's more important to eat.'

The women embroider themes of ploughing the earth and sowing the seed, or carrying heavy water jars on the head and milling the maize with big pestles and mortars – which is women's labour. As well as forming pictures to hang on the wall, the motifs decorate blouses and bags, and adorn stoles with 'the fruit of the earth and the work of human hands'. And in these last weeks the Paraguayan post office has given a boost to Santa María's morale by selecting our nativity wall hangings for their edition of special Christmas stamps: María and José are in traditional folk-dance costume and the baby is slung in a hammock between palm trees.

Our women were rather baffled by it all, never having received a letter in their lives and not knowing what a stamp was. But when they were presented with their complimentary sheets of stamps, they were thrilled, and even more so when they had taken in the explanation that these could be exchanged for real money. Their earnings in recent months have been only between £6 and £9 a month, for four hours' work every day, but they are just beginning to try to reach out to an international market that can pay a little more, offering a mail order facility from the website *www.santamariadefe.com.*

Sometimes the theme of the craft is not just toil but a black and fearful experience, only redeemed by being remembered in the light of Christ. Under President Stroessner, Santa María suffered a fierce persecution of its *Ligas Agrarias Cristianas*, which were founded in the neighbouring town of Santa Rosa at about the same date as the earliest basic Christian communities of Brazil. This year – 27 years later – the women have begun to tell the story of the repression in appliqué pictures. Paraguay is not the first country to have this idea: in Chile the mothers of the disappeared began to sew their sad story as a political protest and a form of therapy at the same time, and the pictures were called *arpilleras*. The custom also spread to Peru, Bolivia and Colombia.

The Agrarian Leagues used traditional Guaraní names. *Minga* meant joining together to work each other's fields in turn, so that the labour became lighter and more sociable. *Jopói* meant sharing, and we see in the picture different families bringing chickens and cooking pots for a common meal. All the life of the Leagues was based in their biblical reflection, and Jesus appears in the circle as a *campesino* in a yellow shirt with a small cross on it – and with bare feet and *sombrero*.

The Agrarian Leagues began their own schools, which were regarded as provocative by a government that sought to indoctrinate a passive population. Yet today many of the ideas promoted by the *escuelitas campesinas* are incorporated into the post-dictatorship Educational Reform: self-expression, thinking for yourself, valuing local culture, and the use of the Guaraní language. The appliqué pictures show how the children were encouraged to come to school just as they were, barefoot and with patched clothes, instead of having to hide their poverty behind expensive uniform and shoes.

The last two pictures of the series were bravely designed by the wife of one of the community leaders who was imprisoned for several years. There is the night arrest, when a jeep comes by the light of the moon to carry off the men from their homes. The women are left helpless, and the dog barks in vain. Finally there is the torture, when the police kick their prisoners on the ground and hit them with an instrument which has three rubber thongs tipped with metal.

In Santa María it is still hard to talk about these events, because the village was divided into victims and perpetrators. When the tertiary-education Institute put on a dramatization about how the *escuelitas campesinas* were destroyed, the primary headmistress lodged a formal complaint: her father had been one of the policemen involved. But when the liberation theologian, Margot Bremer, saw the hangings of the Agrarian Leagues she said, 'This is the way to remember. No one could live with photographs of torture on their walls, but by turning these experiences into works of art, the story can be told to our children.'

(*First published 24 January 2004.*)

27

No water

As Lent began this year and Jesus went into the desert, the people of Santa María went through their own trial: living without water. The pump broke early one Saturday morning, and someone had to go to Asunción to buy a new one. But Saturday is a half day, Sunday is the day of rest, and Monday happened to be a national holiday. So no water for three days.

I have often been told of prisoners having to survive on a litre of water a day, and it never sounded too impossible, until I was forced to try it. I regularly keep a few bottles stored for the many days here when the water fails (usually because a pipe needs to be mended) but normally the taps run again after a few hours. On this long weekend of trial, some friends brought me a further six litres of water from the bottom of the hill, where the water still flowed without the pump. But still it was not enough.

Water-carrying is a traditional *campesino* activity, and many of my friends are adept at twisting a piece of cloth into a coil – the *apyterao*– to cushion the big clay jar on their head. The embroidered wall hangings in our craft workshop feature women carrying water from the spring, and there is a traditional folk dance where the girls dance with water jars. It always looks so pretty, but the reality is hard. Within a day I had used all my six litres, even though I was the only person in my household and I was trying to be miserly.

Why was it so hard? Thirst was not actually the worst problem, for along the lines of 'let them eat cake' I could drink Coca Cola. As we all know, it flows in abundance all over the globe, and is plenteous in the little corner shop opposite my house. I may not like what it stands for, but since I am not living on a dollar a day like many of my neighbours, I can afford it.

Milk is cheaper than Coca Cola, but there is a catch. You have to boil or pasteurise the milk, and then you need plentiful water to wash up the saucepan where the fatty residue of the milk clings. On this day, when I had boiled my milk I just left the pan in the sink. I tipped the dirty water from the things that were easier to wash into the receptacles that were harder to wash. The liquid was opaque and swimming with food particles, but at least it would help them soak. I reduced cooking to a minimum to save on washing up.

Normally the first thing I would do in the morning is water my garden before the fierce sun rises above the trees. Not today: the marrow and strawberry plants would just have to shrivel. Next I customarily sit in the shade to the left of the house and do my Bible meditation. But now I was impeded by the stink drifting out of the bathroom window. Happy are they in these days who have just a *baño común* – a 'common bathroom', or hole in the ground in a shed at the end of the garden. I quickly used up two litres of water in my non-*baño-común* with only moderate effect, and chucking down a third and a fourth seemed to make no difference at all.

But worst of all was the sticky, horrid feeling of a night's sweat when there is no shower. I suppose you can swill over your body with just half a litre if you don't use soap, but I used a full litre putting on soap and washing it off again. At least I felt a lot better afterwards.

During the day I took to washing my hands like the priest at Mass, with just the fingertips in the water. I became aware of how scurfy my hair had become, but it would have to wait. Every time I washed a cup or a plate, I used the minimum and let the tea towel get dirty instead of wasting water. The floorcloth thick with red polish stood stiffly awaiting a good rinse.

I ran out of ice, but it takes two hands to fill up the polythene ice bags under the tap, and would need three or four hands to tilt bottles of water to fill them. I found a family of little cockroaches had hatched out and were running round the kitchen. I would have zapped them if I had had water to wash the surfaces clean of the poison afterwards, but now I just let them run.

None of my economies were a solution, merely a postponement of the need for water. And when I did go to renew my six bottles of water from down the hill – what we call the *orilla* or the margin where the poorest live – my back and shoulders ached from the weight of carrying them back in my rucksack.

When Jesus said, 'The water that I will give will become a spring of water gushing up to eternal life', the Samaritan woman answered, 'Sir, give me this water, that I may never be thirsty or have to keep coming here to draw water' (*John 4.14–15*). It was not a stupid or ignorant reply after all, but just what I would have said, and many millions of others too, who do not have running water.

(*First published 27 March 2004.*)

28

Harp

I have a new love. My harp. I have long admired Paraguayan harps – the traditional instrument of the country ever since the Jesuit Antonio Sepp introduced it to the Guaraní reductions in Misiones around 1700. After living here for four years I finally decided to buy one, so that other people could play it for me. After all, I do not have time to learn. Or so I thought until I got it. Now it is in my possession, I cannot keep my fingers off it.

Buying a harp, like every other task in Paraguay, is a bit of a challenge. If I were buying something of this size and quality in Europe I could look at a picture on the internet or in a catalogue, pay over the phone, and have it delivered to my door. In Paraguay every transaction has to be made face to face with cash. Fortunately in this case I knew the ropes of the music shops, having accompanied a local musician a couple of years ago buying guitars on behalf of the Santa Maria Education Fund.

The recommended place to buy a guitar or a harp is Luque, and most of the Luque harp-makers have their shop on a stretch of noisy road on the way to the airport. Though it is referred to as 'the *Autopista*' (the only one in the country), it is not really a motorway – only a wide road with no hard shoulder, that can take two cars abreast. Sprawled along the edges, open to the dust and howl of traffic, are a dozen or so music shops.

'Buy from the Sanabria family,' was the advice we received the first time round. This was not hard. All the shops along the kerb bore the name Sanabria, each belonging to a different son of the famed manufacturer.

Last week I rang up Pastor Sanabria in advance to ask if he had any of the cheaper harps in stock. The price he had given me two years ago was 900,000 guaraníes or £90, but he told me this had now gone up to £120. He was evidently keen to secure a sale, as he rang me up every day after that to ask when I was coming. In a dead economy where no one has any money to buy anything, people are perpetually poised on the brink of collapse, no matter how good their products.

When I turned up, Pastor put a padlock on his shop, put me in his rickety van, and drove me down the road to his brother Aureliano, who had himself made the three harps in his shop. I had intended to buy the cheapest, undecorated one, but when I saw the harp with hand-carved leaves and flowers – inspired by Jesuit decorative motifs – and heard the richer sonorous tone of the trebo wood compared to the cedar, I was won over and dug out £175 (reduced from £200).

I squeezed the harp into the back seat of a taxi, and then loaded it flat into the luggage compartment of the bus back to Misiones. I was nervous about this as a means of transportation, as the bus lurched at speed round curves on Ruta Uno towards Misiones, and rattled at leisure over cobbles. 'Please God may my harp be all right,' I prayed like a child. But Aureliano Sanabria had assured me it would be fine like that, and it was.

Normally I cannot keep awake on this five-hour journey, but this time I found myself reading the harp manual avidly cover to cover, and in my excitement I did not manage to get off to sleep even when I tried. The Paraguayan harp, I read, is quite different from the modern European variety – which has moved on since the time of the seventeenth-century Jesuits. In Europe, the strings are tighter, more metallic and further apart. In Paraguay, the looser strings give a more sonorous tone. The European harp has pedals to change the key, but the Paraguayan harp is pure wood and is diatonic – and usually tuned to F major. The instrument is simpler and more beautiful to look at, but to make a flat you have to retune the string, or temporally shorten it with the pressure of your finger or of a metal tuning key.

Paraguayan harpists make much use of the *trémulo* technique, especially at the end of a *glizando* – something unknown to Europeans. The European harp is more dependent on the accompaniment of other instruments, while Paraguayan harpists – with more strings within reach – make a single instrument into a whole orchestra, playing the melody with the right hand while harmonies and rhythm flow out of the left hand. Europeans play decorously with the fingers, but Paraguayans pluck vigorously with the fingertips and nails, in the manner of 'an aggressive cat'. The sound that emerges is more energetic and more complete in itself: recordings of Paraguayan music often feature a single harp played on its own, and performing seemingly astonishing feats.

I arrived home with my harp in the late afternoon, and that night was my birthday party. When the group of musicians turned up with guitars and accordion, the talented Nani inaugurated my harp with great panache to an audience of 80 friends in my moonlit garden, as we danced the polka. Nani has never been able to afford his own harp, nor has he ever had a harp lesson in his life, nor can he even read music. But boy, can he play!

(*First published 24 July 2004.*)

ൠൠ   ฅฅ

A Tablet *reader kindly bought a harp for Nani after this piece was published. He has made ample use of it, and six years later graduated to a new harp, while his original harp has passed on to one of the young harp students who have classes funded by the Santa María Education Fund.*

29

Ycuá Bolaños

On the corner of the roads Santísima Trinidad and Artigas in Asunción is a huge and grandiose building with a tall tower, like a cathedral. It is named after a remarkable Franciscan friar, Luis Bolaños, who miraculously made a spring of water arise from the ground with a blow of his staff – 'Bolaños Spring', or in Guaraní *Ycuá Bolaños*. But Ycuá Bolaños in Asunción is not a cathedral. It is a supermarket, which burned down on 1 August 2004 with 400 people inside.

The deaths happened because the management gave the orders to lock the fire doors after the fire started, to prevent looting. I know one of the firefighters – a volunteer fireman from Santa María who was called up with his team to the capital city, four hours' drive away. I knew one of the victims, too. His name was Mario, and I have a postcard he sent me after my first visit to Paraguay. He was a Jesuit novice at that time, though he later left and became a teacher. On the fateful day he had taken his pupils to the cafeteria of Ycuá Bolaños. When the fire began he devoted himself to rescuing his pupils. He saved a lot of them, but lost his own life before he could get all of them out. So he died a martyr, giving his life to save others.

With the march of globalisation, more and bigger supermarkets and shopping centres have been built in the capital (though not in the *campo*, where I live), and people are very proud of them, precisely because this is the way the better-off countries live. So near to a European mentality, and yet so far. Nowhere in Europe could people think that the thing to do when you have a fire is to lock the firedoors so that no one can get out. The point of building fire escapes, for the management, was to get permission to open their supermarket, and it had nothing to do with saving people's lives, which was not their concern. This was amply demonstrated by the reported comment of the supermarket owner afterwards, that no one had lost more than he did in the fire, because he had lost all his money.

Now it may well be true that he has lost all his money, for insurance is practically non-existent in Paraguay, and there is no system for coping with bankruptcy. But his openly expressed sense of priorities is as mind-boggling as the instruction to lock the fire escapes. However, if the supermarket owner didn't care, the rest of the city of Asunción did, as is shown in this poetic reflection by an anonymous author, which dropped on my email mat just after the fire:

———————

How different everything is. The streets of Asunción are gloomy and solitary, and it is as though everything has stopped for a moment, as though we are waiting to wake up from a nightmare. The silence is stunning, deafening. The air we breathe is reeking with agony. The faces, as they burned, took command of the winds and shared with us the pain of their death …

There were whole families going to the supermarket of a Sunday to prepare their intimate family lunch. There were celebrations. There were parents bearing home with love the fruit of their sacrifice at work. There were children choosing coloured pencils for their homework. There were mothers choosing the best vegetables for their children. There were children wanting toys. There were dreams. There were projects. There were lives.

I believe we can hear the shouting still: 'Mummy, why did they close the doors?' 'Excuse me, sir, we don't want to steal anything, it's just that we can't breathe, the fire is hurting us!' 'Careful, don't tread on that girl!' 'Open up, please, my children are waiting for me!' 'Open up, please, my family is inside!' …

Entire families took each other by the arms to face the fire, others did it absolutely alone: old people, young people, children; but all united in one sole cry that made the earth tremble and then rose above it, bearing witness to grief, despair and powerlessness.

'OPEN THE DOORS!!!'

And the doors of heaven opened.

Five years later, I took two recently arrived volunteer English-teachers to see the burnt-out shell of Ycuá Bolaños, and they went on talking about it in stunned disbelief for a long time afterwards. Ycuá Bolaños has big round arches – Romanesque arches we could call them – around the entrance to the ground-floor car park. Today they are blackened with soot and surrounded by graffiti: 'We workers will not forget our dead', 'Genocide', 'Silence, never again' and 'Murderer'. In the shell of the building, the victims' families have made a shrine, and it was attended on the day we went by a man whose 26-year-old son had died in the fire. He told us many details I had not heard before.

The fire began, he said, in the chimney of the café. When they had constructed it they found it collided with a structural rib of the building, and they put two right-angle bends to elbow around the obstruction. As a result, every time the chimney was cleaned, the fats got pushed up and around the corner, and eventually these ignited.

The fire began discreetly at 9.00 am, and the customers continued filling the supermarket without any idea of the problem. But the management knew, we were told, because they gave orders to clear the money out of the tills. They saved the money, but made no attempt to clear the building of people. At 11.25 there was a sudden loud explosion, and all the ceilings suddenly shot into flame. At this point the people found they were locked in, and attempts were made by spectators outside to break open escape routes through the windows. But it was impossible, as the building was secure as a fortress, with small panels of glass set in a criss-cross of unbreakable iron bars.

What it must have been like inside is portrayed in a large painting now standing in the ground-floor car park. At one extreme is a sinister beaked figure making off with his suitcase stuffed with money. In the building behind him, flames lick up from the floor and down from the ceiling. A pregnant woman with a cross in her hands kneels and raises her eyes to heaven. A crowd of victims run screaming with their hands lifted high above their heads, but there is nowhere to run to, so they run in circles. Three victims imprisoned by the grid windows scream and cover their eyes from the smarting smoke. Bodies with the clothes burnt off them and wide screaming mouths collapse in the red and orange flames.

Sentences have at last been passed, after five years of huge popular pressure for justice. The owner of the supermarket got twelve years, his son got ten years, and the security guard, who gave the order to lock the doors, got five years.

We went away with figures from the posters graven in our memories: '9 disappeared. 206 orphaned. 400 dead. 1,071 homes destroyed. 69,000 people affected.' This is a cathedral of sorrow that continues to stand today as a witness to the value of human life.

(*From columns first published 28 August 2004 and 28 November 2009.*)

30

Breast cancer

'I have a lump in my breast,' said Epifania, when she came to visit relatives in Santa María. Her sister felt it, and said, 'How big and how hard it is. You must go to the doctor'. I echoed, 'Yes, yes, you must.' Epifania looked unconvinced, though she said, 'It's been there for ages, I'm really quite worried about it.'

It was somehow quite clear that Epifania was never going to go to the doctor. And the reason was not fear, as it would be in Europe. It was money. Not necessarily the cost of the visit itself: you can get a visit to the doctor for as little as 10p if you go to the right person at the right time. It was the knowledge that a visit to the doctor, especially on a matter like that, opens up a long sequence of tests and medicines and further referrals. In no time she would have eaten up what little money she had, and still have fallen far short of the end of the process. She would be left with a sense of failure and embarrassment. And she would be no better.

What is more, she would have a keener sense of what could have been done if only she had not belonged to the excluded class. Better not to know. Better to keep those few precious guaraníes for something that could be afforded, not waste them on a part payment for something that would remain forever outside her reach.

How different it is in the country of my birth. In England, on my annual visit, I did not even have a lump in my breast before the eagle-eyed process of routine over-50s breast screening detected some tiny white flecks. An amazing machine drilled a little hole for a biopsy with microscopic precision, and firm doctors now insist that I cannot return to Paraguay until the cancer has been completely zapped – a process that will delay my return to South America for some months. I may have the minor inconvenience of waiting three months in a queue for non-urgent radiotherapy, but at the end of the day I know that I will receive state-of-the-art analysis and state-of-the-art treatment.

There is the rub, where Latin America lovers like myself abandon our adopted countries. While we try to live like the poor, when it comes to health, we reserve for ourselves privileges that are far beyond their reach. Over the last couple of years I have seen two Jesuit priests pulled out of their Paraguayan ministry to go back to the United States for extensive medical treatment. Happily they have now both returned to Paraguay, with a clean bill of health. When faced with the choice between a £1 tooth extraction in Paraguay or a £60 tooth extraction in England, I do not hesitate to buy British.

The problem comes when you begin to think you deserve these privileges, that for the poor of the south are mind-blowingly generous. Hearing a headline news story about people in the UK lying on beds in ambulances because the beds inside the hospital were full, I found myself annoyed by the whingeing. Do people really think that this is one of the most important things that have happened in the world in the last 24 hours? The petty-mindedness of consumer complaints that hit the headlines is a sign of an unbalanced self-preoccupation, which in its turn – I am sorry to use strong language – implies nationalism and racism. A splinter in a British little finger matters more than the mountains of corpses from medical under-funding in most of the rest of the world.

So far away, and yet so near. Until I return to Paraguay, I will carry the country in my head and in my heart. When my computer goes into idling mode, it flashes up a random selection of my photos, and, finding myself looking involuntarily at some pictures of Santa María the other day, I felt a pang of nostalgia.

There was Karina, the girl who does my laundry, beaming as she hugged her amazingly good-looking toddler, Celeste ('Sky-blue', despite her big brown eyes). They live on the *orilla* –the 'shore' or edge of town – and have only just got their first fragile electric cable strung up, to activate a huge television. It may not be my choice of priorities, but I know nothing else gives them such pleasure.

There was a row of some of my favourite priests, concelebrating Mass in our lovely parish church. It is a building that retains the spirit of traditional Guaraní architecture – an airy space with a roof held up on rough tree-trunk pillars – even though it does not actually date back to the era of the Missions. The church is packed with my friends, and as I looked at the photo I could almost hear the music.

There was a group of young people clapping their hands and singing a song, on the outdoor stage in the square, just one year ago, in the novena leading up the patronal feast of the birth of the Virgin, 8 September. I can recognise most of their faces – some are my students – and their eager energy, in the blackness of the surrounding night, is a reminder of what our world's youth could achieve if we got our priorities right.

(*First published 25 September 2004.*)

I returned to Paraguay with a clean bill of health in May 2005. Epifania never had her breast lump investigated, but she is still alive today so we assume it must be benign.

31

Closing the embassy

'Giving a voice to the voiceless.' We all agree with that. Or do we? Not apparently the British Government, which is closing its embassy in Paraguay, along with eight other diplomatic posts around the world: Vanuatu, Tonga, East Timor, Kiribati, Bahamas, Lesotho, Swaziland and Madagascar.

It is a sock in the eye to Paraguay, but there never is a cloud without a silver lining. Our outspoken Jesuit Pa'i Oliva (Francisco de Paula Oliva) was quick to find one: 'That's one coloniser at a safer distance!'

Pa'i Oliva went on to make another point, half ironically, half seriously: 'We should thank Britain. They have done us the favour of making us think. Do any of us know much about Vanuatu, Tonga? Well, with all due respect to these sister states, Paraguay is on the same level as them.' In fact, with the exception of Madagascar, Paraguay is enormously bigger than all the other countries to lose their embassies.

The closure of these embassies, and some other subordinate posts, will free up six million pounds a year, not counting expenses like redundancy payments. If it is a matter of necessary cost-cutting, the closures might be presented as an unfortunate necessity. But the Foreign Office denied that the motivation was economic. In the last seven years some 500 new Foreign Office jobs have been created, said Baroness Symons, trying to prove that services were improving, not deteriorating. These take priority over our *two* staff jobs in Asunción.

'Our overseas posts are kept under constant review to keep pace with the changing international environment, and it is not necessary to keep these posts open,' a Foreign Office spokesman told me. 'So we don't need an embassy in Paraguay?' I asked, dumbfounded. 'In a nutshell, absolutely,' he confirmed.

So Pa'i Oliva is right, with knobs on. Paraguay is now a totally insignificant country.

Why is it so insignificant? In land mass it is almost double the size of Britain, and it used to be one of the most influential, most powerful, most economically advanced countries in Latin America. It had one of the first railways in the continent – built by British engineers, incidentally. But that all changed in 1864–70, when the country was utterly destroyed by the Triple Alliance War – a war, incidentally, that Paraguayans blame partly on the British wanting to make trading inroads into the country. Paraguay has never received aid for recovery. It has never recovered.

We have often seen at moments of international disaster how enormously generous the British can be when they know other people need their help. But it all depends on communication and awareness. Rather than consigning Paraguay to further invisibility by pulling out our embassy, is it not time we provided some reconstruction money, especially if we are under suspicion (however unfairly) of contributing to the destruction in the first place?

I asked a Foreign Office spokesman what the Government considered the function of an embassy to be. He sounded a bit nonplussed, but offered a few suggestions: to maintain links with the host government; to boost trade; to do visa work and so on; to give consular assistance. I suggested: 'How about to provide information about the country to the British Government to help them shape their foreign policy?' He replied: 'Well that goes without saying. That is the whole point.' Too obvious to mention. Or too obvious to be remembered.

If we want efficiency savings in the Foreign Office budget, we need to keep our eye on that 'whole point', and find other ways of cutting costs. The *Observer* recently reported (*23 January 2005*) that the Foreign Office spends £17 million a year on private school fees for children of diplomats, even though in one-third of cases the parents are living in Britain. And over time I have made my own smaller observations of lavishness.

Do we need, for example, to have such a gorgeous building for an embassy? It adds to British prestige, but how much is that feel-good factor really worth? Is it really necessary that all the electrical fittings have square three-pin plugs and that you can flush paper down the toilet – an unheard-of luxury in Latin America. 'Everything inside the embassy has to be to British Standards,' I was told. Very nice. Really. But is it helping an embassy fulfil its 'whole point' of informing British foreign policy?

And is it necessary to throw lavish diplomatic parties? I went to one at the British embassy in Asunción and it was bizarre. Out of the two UK-based staff, only one attended, and dominant among the local guests seemed to be employees of the British American Tobacco Company (is this our principal trading interest today?) and white-skinned people dressed in smart British clothes who looked the part until they opened their mouths and turned out to be Paraguayans with a British ancestor. One of the British American Tobacco people told me how comfortable life had been under the Stroessner dictatorship, and how Lino Oviedo (a politician-gangster believed by most people to have ordered the assassination of the vice president Luis María Argaña in 1999) had been a regular invitee at all embassy parties until a formal warrant for his arrest had been issued. Does this style of social event really help an embassy to fulfil its 'whole point' of informing British foreign policy?

Paradoxically, even as the announcement was being made of the embassy closure in mid-December 2004, Paraguay was receiving unexpected attention from another British source. The Royal Mail sent all the Christmas cards and parcels addressed to Ascension Island to Asunción by mistake. Oh well, they are both too insignificant to tell them apart.

(*First published 5 February 2005.*)

ॐॐ   ॐॐ

Paraguay is still without a British embassy, even though Fernando Lugo's government has turned Paraguay into a uniquely valuable listening post for the whole South American continent.

32

Jesuits

No one who has seen the film *The Mission* will forget the haunting moment when Fr Gabriel, played by Jeremy Irons, went into the jungle in the midst of a dangerous tribe. Alone and vulnerable, armed with nothing more than an oboe, he sat on a rock and played a tune so sad and poignant that it makes one weep. And it won the hearts of the Guaraní, who were a music-loving people.

What is most extraordinary about this story is how true it was. Jesuits did take their lives in their hands and go into uncharted, indigenous territory, if not alone then in pairs. They did play music in the forest and the Guaraní did come down onto the river banks to listen as their boats drifted by. They did win the hearts of the Guaraní by their gentle, courageous love, by their self-sacrifice, and by their artistic creativity – promoting music and sculpture, architecture and dance. And as much as they were loved by the Guaraní, they were hated by the Spanish and Portuguese colonisers and slave-owners, who eventually, after a struggle of 150 years, succeeded in having them expelled.

There were great heroes among them, but the more you read you the more it seems they were all great heroes. They were an army, the Company of Jesus, with a common mission and a common strategy to achieve it. 'Does gold come before souls?' was their rallying cry, as they fought with the church authorities for permission to work in the dangerous, isolated areas that were to become Paraguay, instead of gold-rich Peru. They won the argument, swayed the policy at the epoch-making Synod of Asunción, 1603, and established the missionary principles that priests should learn Guaraní and give all instruction in the native language, and that the indigenous people should be physically protected from – and separated from – the European exploiters.

And so the 'reductions' or mission settlements were born, of which Santa María de Fe was one. Their aim was to provide a place where the Guaraní could marry each other, instead of providing bedmates for the Europeans; could work for their own prosperity, instead of providing slave-labour for the Europeans; and could be educated in their own language – even learning to read and write in it – instead of seeing it die off as their culture was over run. Despite these efforts, as many as half a million Guaraní were captured and sold in the slave markets of São Paulo, some of them marched away in chains as their Jesuit friends ran alongside the convoy and pleaded with the Portuguese for their release.

The Guaraní loved the reductions, and the Jesuits could scarcely found them fast enough for them. It was an austere life in the beginning, and the founding Fathers were, according to a contemporary account, 'desperately poor, but rich in enthusiasm: their garments were so patched that there was no sign of the original material, and their shoes were mended with pieces of cloth that they had cut off the bottom of their soutanes'. They made a six-litre flagon of wine last them for nearly five years, so they could keep on saying Mass.

Over the years – the experiment lasted for 150 years in all – the reductions became productive centres of farming where both the faith and the arts flourished. We hear the names of a number of remarkably talented Jesuits who sacrificed their lives in Europe to live and die in South America. (In those days there was no flying to and fro, and many of those who volunteered died on the voyage out, without even beginning to work.) There was Giuseppe Brassanelli, the sculptor, whose work can still be seen in the museums of Misiones; Giovanni Bautista Primoli, the architect, thanks to whom we have the ruins of Trinidad, a world heritage site; Domenico Zipoli, the composer, considered in Italy a rival of Vivaldi, before he gave everything up to go and bury himself in South

America; Anton Sepp, the diarist, constructor of musical instruments, and writer of plays in Guaraní.

If these Jesuits were considerable artists, there were other Jesuits who were quite simply saints. Roque González de Santa Cruz is one of three officially canonised Paraguayan Jesuits. Son of a Spanish father and an indigenous mother, he joined the diocesan clergy first, but became a Jesuit to avoid the ecclesial promotions that were coming his way and that would take him away from work among the people. He then went unarmed and Jeremy-Irons-like, into a fiercely dangerous tribe – not the Guaraní but the Guaycurú – with just one companion. It was nearly 20 years later and in a different region that he was murdered by a witchdoctor, after founding ten reductions.

The provincial who sent him out, Diego de Torres, was a man of uncompromising commitment who prayed for four hours every day. He struggled against enormous opposition to achieve the release of slaves and forced labourers, but the cause was deeply controversial. 'Even if he had done nothing else with his whole life than begin this admirable venture,' wrote one historian, 'Diego de Torres would have sufficient claim to the whole world's admiration as being one of the great benefactors of humanity.' An Italian cardinal, who made a general confession to him, said that if he were ever made Pope he would make the faith penetrate to the far corners of the universe under the direction of de Torres.

Possibly the most brilliant of all, and the best known after San Roque González, was Antonio Ruiz de Montoya, another son of a Spanish father and an indigenous mother, but this time of Peruvian origin, and illegitimate. He had a rowdy and misspent youth, to the point of being involved in a homicide – and so was the inspiration for the Rodrigo Mendoza figure in *The Mission,* played by Robert de Niro. But after a profound conversion and a 30-day retreat, he became passionately determined to join the group of young Jesuits setting out under de Torres for the uncharted territories of Paraguay.

He personally founded 11 reductions, and led a dramatic exodus of 12,000 Guaraní from an area attacked by slave-traders, in search of safer territory 1,000 miles away, on the other side of the mighty Guairá waterfalls. He was the greatest advocate of the Guaraní before the Spanish crown, and wrote the classic history, *La Conquista Espiritual del*

Paraguay, as well as the Guaraní grammar that became the basis for all future work on the language.

If it were not for the Jesuits like Montoya, with their grammars, vocabularies, catechisms and advocacy, Guaraní would not have survived to become the widespread language it is today – the national language of Paraguay alongside Spanish. If it were not for the Jesuits of the present, Guaraní would not be making the further strides it is still making, with international committees working to standardise the differing spelling methods, and popular radio schools teaching adult literacy deep into the *campo,* through the Jesuit-run project *Fe y Alegría.* The best Guaraní dictionary today is by a Jesuit, the best Guaraní grammar is by a Jesuit, and the only complete Guaraní translation of the Bible is by a Jesuit – published less than ten years ago. The mission of uniting scholarship with option for the poor goes on, and is a peculiarly Jesuit charism.

(*First published 26 March 2005.*)

33

Hidden treasure

'It's surprising to think of someone like you going to live in a backwater.'
The comment by an English friend made me think. I do not think of
Santa María de Fe, Paraguay, as a backwater. I think of it as where the real
action is.

What is a backwater? If a backwater is a place hidden away where few
people go, then that is what Santa María is. But I know that will change. A
place as rich as this in history and art and culture cannot lie undiscovered
for long in today's world, and I am blessed to discover it while it is still
unspoilt.

Rather than a backwater, the image that has best described Santa
María to me is the treasure hidden in a field. In Spanish, *campo* means
both 'countryside' and 'field'. So when Matthew speaks of the Reign of
Heaven being like 'a treasure hidden in a field' (*Matthew 13.44*), the
translation could also mean 'a treasure hidden in the countryside', and
that is what Santa María has meant to me. It is something hidden away
that I discovered and wanted, and that I left my previous life to obtain.

Ironically, in the Jesuit era the envious Spaniards believed that there
must be hidden gold mines in Misiones, to explain the economic success
of the reductions. They expelled the Jesuits, searched for the gold, and of
course found nothing. The treasure was there, but was not to be found in
gold.

What I have found in Santa María is a whole world. People in Europe may understand the charm of the simple life, but they may not realize quite how much intellectual satisfaction I also find in this place. Among many towering figures in the group of Jesuit founding fathers, Santa María had its own Jesuit intellectual, Anton Sepp of the Tyrol – a prolific writer whose diaries, letters and books form one of the principal sources for life in the reductions, and an outstanding musician who constructed the first pedal organ in South America, and is known as the father of the harp.

Our next distinguished intellectual was the well-known French botanist, Aimé Jacques Bonpland (1773–1858), who lived for 10 years in Santa María, doing agricultural and medicinal work, and fathering the family of descendants who now bear the rather un-Spanish surname Jacquet, derived from his second Christian name. Before he came to Santa María, he travelled all over South America with his German friend, Alexander von Humboldt, producing drawings of plants and insects. He created a herbarium of more than 60,000 specimens, representing some 6,000 species, half of which he was classifying for the first time. There is a *Museo de Ciencias Naturales Dr Amado Bonpland* in Corrientes, Argentina.

The intellectual heritage of Paraguay was squandered, not only by the expulsion of the Jesuits in 1768, which meant the destruction of the Misiones region, but for a second time by the War of the Triple Alliance in 1864–70, which meant the destruction of everything else in the country, and from which Paraguay has never recovered. Today, the academic standards in the schools and universities of Paraguay are far behind those of modern Europe or North America. Yet there can be more intellectual satisfaction in living in a country where the publication of a book – any book – is an event, so that you have some hope of being up-to-date with the latest thinking, than in living in a world where you are drowned in a sea of paper that dulls the senses and leads to a numbing paralysis of the brain.

Intellectuals are thin on the ground, but they do exist. The late Augusto Roa Bastos, who died on 26 April 2005, was one. 'He's a genius,' said a young friend of mine. Yet the subject of his renowned novel *Hijo de Hombre* ('Son of Man') was simply the everyday life of the *campo* where he grew up. My ageing friend Secundino Núñez in Asunción is another –

a retired priest, journalist, politician and polymath, one of the country's most respected intellectuals and the philosophy teacher of generation after generation passing through the universities of Asunción and Ciudad del Este. Yet he grew up in a simple Guaraní-speaking family, and would walk the fields for an hour to get home from the nearest bus stop, saying his rosary the while.

In Santa María we had another glimpse of the intellectual life, when a distinguished guest lecturer gave the first of several days' teaching at our Institute (where poor students study without paying fees, thanks to the generosity of *Tablet* readers). Carlos Bedoya began his life in a small corner shop – 'my parents began their business with nothing more than a bag of maize' – and is now Professor of History at the Catholic University in San Ignacio, a painter and art-restorer, with degrees in pedagogy, economics and law, and a wealth of prizes to his name.

Bedoya spoke with the sweep and the energy of a hurricane, covering the history of the world in five hours, from the Stone Age to the internet. The students were enthralled, sitting in a big circle on our big veranda, with the sun-speckled garden behind them and the blackboard in front of them, and at the end they were crying out for more. They wrote in their evaluations: 'This man really knows what he is talking about.' 'Never have I heard history so impressive and beautiful.' 'This did not send me to sleep as my secondary school teachers did.' 'Please can we have more.' 'I learned things that were beyond my imagination, and I hope that you will be able to come again to share your incredible knowledge.'

And so the treasure in the *campo* is beginning to be found again, in the gold of faith and learning.

(*First published 30 July 2005.*)

෨෬   ෩෨

Secundino Núñez died on 24 May 2011, the day this book was submitted to the publishers.

34

Identity card

I have an achievement to announce: I have completed the long process of registering as a Paraguayan resident. It has taken me five years and four months to get my *cédula* or identity card, and I am feeling very pleased with myself.

Isn't it strange? When I am in England I think identity cards are an odious intrusion and an affront to civil liberty, but in Paraguay I am proud to carry one. I am regularly asked to give its number, which is 5,165,397 – meaning I am the five millionth and something person to be issued with a *cédula*. Small country.

A *cédula* means you exist. Some of the very poor do not have one – my pretty young deaf-and-dumb friend, Nilsa, for example, did not have one for a long time, because her parents had not been able to pay for it. So when we reflected in my base community on Mary's journey to Bethlehem to be enrolled, I likened the biblical census to getting a *cédula*. Even the poorest people – babies born in stables – had the right to be counted, and even the most important people – the family of the king of the Jews – had to go through the wearing business of travelling and queuing to get their name in the official paperwork.

Why did it take so long to get my *cédula*? A government note I read before I moved to Paraguay said that immigrants from other nations were welcome and the formalities were easy. Not so: I found the process so draining and dismaying that I almost felt like giving up and going back to Britain again.

To get a *cédula* I had first to get a permanent resident's card, and to get that I had first to get a temporary resident's card, which required a plethora of documents, stamps, more stamps, and more stamps, official translations, and at every step a fee. It cost hundreds of pounds. Then begins the wait: a temporary resident's card takes a year to come through, unless you offer a bribe, but being British I looked down my nose at such cheating.

'Why does it take so long?' I protested. 'Because we are up to here in applications,' the official said, gesturing above her head. I did not believe this, as the only people I had seen in the office of *Migraciones* were a few scattered missionaries and a few scattered embassy staff. 'Isn't there any way you can hurry it up?' I complained. She lowered her voice and said, 'I can ask upstairs, but they will want to know how much you are offering.' I told her I had not meant it that way.

When a year had passed and they still would not give me my resident's card I lost my temper, and it worked like magic. They put me down as having made a complaint, and a month later I had the card. 'Nobody gets their card until they make an official complaint,' confided the woman at the desk *sotto voce* after she had handed it over to me. It would have been helpful to know that in advance.

To get my permanent resident's card, another year on, I had to pass a medical check and either have a work contract or a deposit of $5,000 in a Paraguayan bank account. I put in the necessary sum and took my new bank statement along. The woman behind the desk looked at it as though she had never seen a bank statement before, which was probably the case. 'This is no good, it does not even have a signature,' she said. I went back to the bank, where they pointed out to me that bank statements never have signatures. However, they agreed to sign it if that would help.

The medical check at the Ministry of Health was quite fun. A doctor looked at my skin and certified that I did not have leprosy. Another did a chest x-ray and certified that I did not have tuberculosis. Another printed out my heart rate and certified that I was not about to drop down dead. Another did a blood test and certified that I did not have AIDS. And finally, a psychologist asked me what I thought of US foreign policy and certified that I showed no signs of madness.

With all these documents safely deposited in *Migraciones,* I waited the regulation year and then made an official complaint, and so got my permanent resident's card. I was now eligible to apply for a *cédula.* After a new sequence of visits to different offices to receive new stamps and pay new fees, I was ready to have my photo and fingerprints taken, at the hurly burly of *Identificaciones,* along with all the other Paraguayans.

Now if I had my fingerprints taken in Britain I would feel ashamed and embarrassed. But in Paraguay it feels perfectly fine, as everyone is queuing up to have it done. The officials are very practised at seizing and rolling your inky fingers exactly into the ten spaces on the card in a jiffy. Then you spend rather longer washing the ink off your fingers in some very blackened basins with some very blackened soap.

The *cédula* came, but it had my surname misspelled (for which I can hardly blame them, with a surname like mine). I had to have a new photograph, and new fingerprints. Several more useless trips later to see why the card had not arrived, they figured out that I had been photographed on the day when the camera was not working. I had to have my photograph taken again, and wait once more for the process to take its course. But in December I got my correct *cédula* at last. Now I can vote in elections, and sit back and relax, until it runs out on 7 December 2015.

(*First published 7 January 2006.*)

 C3C3   80ε0

These processes are improving in Paraguay. My son got his cédula with rather less hassle, but still some hassle.

35

Immigrants and emigrants

I was a bit tickled recently to be invited to a 'day for immigrants'. I associate immigrants with exploited, undervalued people on the outskirts of society. Not in Paraguay. Immigrants are more often the people who run things.

The immigrant hosting the day was a Peruvian, who runs a Country Club with saunas and tennis courts. Other guests included a German, who is in charge of the department of public works for his local municipality, some East-Europeans from a wealthier part of the region, and a Brazilian, who is an irrigation advisor to the agricultural sector.

While we immigrants were living it up with a barbecue by the tennis courts, thousands of poor Paraguayans were setting out to try to become immigrants in other countries. For years they have been flooding into Buenos Aires. I have always found it depressing to see some of our brightest young people laying aside their educational aspirations to serve as cleaning ladies in a foreign land.

But now a new drain has got under way in alarming proportions: the flight to Spain. People go as tourists, look for work, and hope to end up as legal residents. How many actually succeed in this last aspiration is unclear. Sometimes it is a disaster. A friend told me of a qualified dentist she knows who took out a big loan to pay her fare to Spain, and now finds herself doing miserably paid domestic work, with insufficient income to pay her way back to Paraguay, let alone repay her debt.

Santa María has her share of these new voyagers, whose fares are paid by a family member who has gone ahead of them. So one immigrant gives birth to another. I stressed to the mother of one would-be Spanish adventurer the folly of living in Europe illegally. Her justification was a very simple one: 'Everyone is doing it. Everyone.' Of course, it is natural to think there must be safety in numbers.

The numbers going to Spain now are so great that Spain has put pressure on Paraguay to hold back the floodgates. The number of people applying for passports has trebled in two years. (Paraguayans do not need a passport to go to Argentina.) So Paraguay has suspended the issue of passports, except in cases of genuine necessity. This might have seemed a good idea, but it has caused chaos.

As it happens, I have been helping one of my students to get a passport in these last weeks – not to go to Spain, but to Scotland, as a volunteer with the Iona Community. Fabiana went prepared with letters of recommendation from the local government to argue her case, and found an office filled with distressed and tearful applicants. One person was unable to go to her mother on her death bed. Another was unable to go to her son who had had a serious accident. In this atmosphere of desperation, corruption flourishes, and in no time Fabiana was offered a passport if she would pay two million guaraníes (£200).

The saga of Fabiana's passport went on for weeks, till I lost count of the number of needless journeys she made, even though I was paying for them – not to mention the hours spent trying to get through on the phone, only to be told that her passport was expected next Tuesday, or by the end of the week, or tomorrow. And tomorrow. And tomorrow. When she travelled up, she would go on the night bus, arriving at 5.00 am at the bus terminal after a cold and sleepless night. She would get to the passport office two hours before it opened, and wait in the winter cold on the pavement with a headache.

The Director's secretary, who was supposed to be helping her, seemed to be avoiding talking to her, but while she was waiting, Fabiana talked with someone who had got his passport through after paying this same secretary two installments of 600,000 (£60, at that date). It is such an easy way of making a lot of money, that the staff convince themselves there is nothing wrong in it: they are only helping people in need (goes the thinking), and it is reasonable to expect a tip.

Eventually, after Fabiana had waited two whole days on end in the crowded office, she rang me at 7.30 pm at night to say she had the passport in her hand. She had only got it, she told me, because she found an honest policeman who told her it was ready. The others were not bothering to look for it, because she was not paying them.

Later in the week a television channel did some undercover reporting with hidden cameras of a passport received for a bribe of a million guaraníes. The passport came through – from initial application to finished book in hand – in 24 hours.

(*First published 3 June 2006.*)

 মৈমৈ ৰহৰ

Passports usually come through now in three weeks without a problem.

36

Boquerón

I have never liked the idea of visiting a war site, particularly the site of a glorified national event. So I was surprised by the impact made on me by Boquerón, famed for the victory that set the way for Paraguay's defeat of Bolivia in the 1932–5 Chaco War. The victory of Boquerón is celebrated in Paraguay as an annual national holiday.

The Chaco covers more than half of Paraguay's territory but contains only 2 per cent of its population. The fort of Boquerón is deep in the midst of this inhospitable and barren land, difficult of access and hard to find. It was important to the two warring sides because it had a lake (not much more than a pond really), providing water in the heart of the desert.

A notice placed at the entrance by the pacifist Mennonite group that now owns the land calls it 'a Bolivian fort taken by the Paraguayan troops on 29 September 1932'. But that annoys the Paraguayan visitors, who insist it was a Paraguayan fort, taken by the Bolivians and then taken back again.

As the war raged, thirst became a worse threat than armaments. Paraguayan soldiers crazed with thirst would race under enemy fire to get to the borders of the lake, only to be shot down as they reached the brink, their dead bodies polluting the precious water. Other soldiers would plead with their commanding officers to let them have a few sips of their urine. And many shot themselves in the left hand, to earn a place in hospital where there was water, until the authorities got wise to the number of similar injuries.

Both Paraguay and Bolivia believe that the Chaco was originally theirs, but for a long time it did not particularly matter which map version was taken as authoritative, since no one – apart from a few hardy indigenous groups – wanted to live there. The war only broke out when it was rumoured that the Chaco contained oil. Sometimes Britain and the USA are blamed for fomenting it, through rival oil companies.

For Paraguay the war had symbolic motivations too, because the country had been utterly destroyed in its previous conflict – the Triple Alliance War of 1864–70, against Brazil, Argentina and Uruguay – and the people felt the need to restore national dignity. But what use has Paraguay made of the Chaco subsequently? None. The oil has not materialised, and if you ask you are told that the only viable oil is in the part of the Chaco handed back to Bolivia in the 1938 peace accord, which was forced on to Paraguay under international pressure.

Today Boquerón is visited by many school parties from Paraguay, but sadly none from Bolivia. Yet the layout of the site is tasteful and respectful, and the overall mood is more tragic than triumphant. You will find a plaque giving 'Glory and honour to the fallen', but it is planted in the midst of a purple-flowering cactus. Inside the museum of rusty battle relics is a tribute of 'Eternal gratitude to the heroes of the Chaco!' from a Paraguayan school, but alongside it is a framed text placed by the pacifist Mennonite colony of Neuland (the owners of the land today) that reads: 'Paraguay, America and the World should learn from their history that wars impoverish populations and sow hatred amongst people. No more war and violence between brothers!'

The most visually memorable monument is the stainless steel soldier running on a hillside, the work of artist Herman Guggiari. He has a large hole in his chest where his heart should be – it is the shape of the map of Paraguay. Another memorial is a stone bas relief frieze showing a line of the people involved in the war: soldiers with swords and cannons are followed up by a nurse tending the wounded, a priest reading the funeral prayers, and a woman and child trailing behind with some meagre provisions.

But the monument that I liked best was placed in 2004 by the Presidents of both Paraguay and Bolivia. Two huge stainless steel leaves representing the two countries at war, ripple in parallel, not touching, and a plaque renders 'homage to the fallen, who in offering their blood constructed the foundations of peace and fraternity that today unite our peoples'. The truth is that even today there is little communication between the two neighbouring countries – the arid Chaco acting as an impenetrable barrier between them.

The casualties were massive. Nearly 100,000 died, with Bolivia suffering slightly more losses than Paraguay.

Whatever the truth, the layout of Boquerón tells a grisly tale. The fort is surrounded by a four-kilometre circle of trenches, with lookout posts every five metres from where the Bolivians shot down the approaching Paraguayan troops. The only way the Paraguayans could take the fort was by crossing a treeless field where there was no cover, other than by piling up in front of them the gunned-down bodies of their companions. It took 8,000 Paraguayans 20 days of such carnage to defeat 1,200 Bolivians. The Paraguayans inched forward behind walls of flesh three bodies high, and took the fort on 29 September 1932.

The Paraguayan cemetery is placed in this field, where most of them died, and a mass of tightly spaced white crosses indicate where there was a huge common grave. The Bolivian cemetery is placed inside the trenches, where most of them died.

In the tragic folly of this historic site, one contemporary sign of sanity and hope shines out: a twin grave where a Paraguayan and a Bolivian lie buried together. Captain Tomas Manchego of Bolivia and First Lieutenant Fernando Velázquez of Paraguay became friends when Manchego was a prisoner in Paraguay, prior to the formal outbreak of war. They met again in a Bolivian hospital, when both men were dying from their wounds, and the two left instructions that after their death their bodies were to be buried in a joint grave. By some miracle, this wish was respected, despite an attempt by Bolivia to reclaim Manchego's body a couple of years ago, and the witness of that grave with its simple tree-trunk headstone and two little flags painted on the same piece of wood brings a drop of sanity into a field of tragic sadness.

(*First published 29 July 2006.*)

37

Santa María Hotel

I had passed the roughly hand-painted sign 'land for sale' innumerable times before I acted. I think it was there for four years in all, and the land did not sell, not because no one wanted it but because no one in Santa María de Fe had the money to buy it. The site could not have been better – right on the historic square of this pretty little town that was once a famous Jesuit Mission for the Guaraní.

At first I just ignored the sign, as part of the background scenery. It did not concern me, for I believed that Paraguayan land should be owned by Paraguayans, not by foreigners. But as time went by I found myself thinking, each time I passed, 'This little town needs a hotel, and that is where it should be: right on the square, looking out on the museum and the church and the foundational cross, in the shadow of the trees where our friendly family of monkeys live.' Then I thought, 'But it will never happen, because in Paraguay there is never money to invest in anything.'

Later on I began to think, 'If I don't build it then it won't happen. Or, worse, it will be built by some big foreign company that moves in and does it in a way that spoils our lovely little town and exploits the people's heritage. It will be like so many other national assets that have been privatised into foreign hands.'

I never dreamt, when I went to live in Santa María, that I would become a hotel proprietor, and I am looking for an early opportunity to step out of that role. A few years ago I would have been horrified by the idea of starting up a business, with its overtones of the nasty capitalist world; but today I believe that analysing why the poor are poor implies being prepared to do something practical about it, and no better way than by starting a business. I have set up the Santa María Hotel with the pledge that all profits will go to the local people, although it had to be registered in my name at the start to get it going.

The Santa María museum is considered by many people to be the finest of all the museums of the 30 Jesuit-Guaraní reductions. Many people also consider that as a town Santa María is the most attractive of those 30 towns today, for its peace and tranquillity and the way the present-day community continues to be centred around the original square.

Yet of all the 30 towns that have something remaining, Santa María has the fewest visitors. San Ignacio Miní in Argentina gets some 20 or more busloads of visitors each day. Santa María de Fe can sometimes go a full month without a single busload. By consequence, it has the least money circulating, the fewest jobs, and the greatest poverty. Part of the reason for the dearth of visitors is the lack of tourist information, and another part is – or, rather, *was* – the lack of a place to stay.

At the new Santa María Hotel (*www.santamariahotel.org*) those students who have been working hard at their English for the last four or five years suddenly find their skills have a practical application as they welcome overseas guests. For the moment we are a very tiny project – with just three double rooms, the right size for a family or two – but small seeds can grow, and this one is already growing. We have successfully managed to accommodate a pilgrimage group of 11, putting half the visitors in family homes where they formed affectionate relationships with the local *campesinos*, and meeting all together at the hotel for meals.

A key principle is that the project should be locally owned and run for the benefit of the local people. That benefit is clearly economic in the first instance, but it does not end there, because visitors are asked to come 'in a spirit of pilgrimage', and that leads to a faith-sharing that is mutually beneficial.

'A spirit of pilgrimage' does not necessarily mean that visitors have to be Christians, let alone Catholics, but it does mean that visitors should come with respect for the *campesinos* and their simple traditional life, with a desire to learn from them, and with an openness to the well of spirituality that is to be found here.

That was the spirit that led someone in our first pilgrimage group of 11 to lead a mixed group of visitors and locals in Tai Chi every morning in the centre of the square. And it was the spirit that took them on a two-hour trip to our local Calvary hill riding in an ox cart – an excursion that has been repeated with a number of visitors, who love the slow-moving meditative movement of the cart.

The rooms are named after famous Jesuits – Roque González, Sepp, Montoya – and every one has a carved stone slab set in the wall, copied from carvings in the Ruins. There is a little chapel at the end of the garden, built as the simplest, poorest homes are built, with wood tree-trunk walls and a thatched roof. There is a library housing my collection of books on the Jesuit-Guaraní reductions, turning this into a study centre as well as a hotel.

Artisans from Santa María have embroidered the curtains and made the shades for the bedside lamps, while the woven bedspreads and rugs and hammocks come from nearby San Miguel, originally part of Santa María's terrain before it became a separate *municipio*. The plates are made by a potter in Areguá (slightly farther afield) and the wooden leather-thonged furniture is made in the Pa'i Pukú school in the Chaco, a project of the Jesuit-run Fe y Alegría project for educating the poor.

What we are trying to do – and according to our guests we are succeeding – is to build a bridge between foreign visitors and the local poor. The Hotel is a springboard for visiting the old Jesuit sites; but it is also a point of insertion for meeting the local people, and for visiting their projects.

(*First published 14 October 2006.*)

38

Chiquitos

Sometimes I dream about what Santa María would have been like when it was still a Jesuit-Guaraní reduction, in the age that has been called in a number of book titles 'The Lost Paradise', 'The Vanished Arcadia', '150 Years of Happiness'. The expulsion of the Jesuits from Latin America in 1768 marked a sudden end to that golden age of art and music and hard-working community life inspired by faith.

The Guaraní Republic of 30 mission towns for the indigenous, from which Europeans were excluded, had been so successful that it was destroyed out of jealousy. It may sound ridiculous, but the Spanish and Portuguese were convinced that its economic success was due to secret gold mines, and when they drove the Jesuits out they lopped the heads off the statues in the hope that they would find gold hidden within.

What would Santa María have been like when the bells still called the Guaraní to Mass, and they sang the music of the Jesuit composer, Domenico Zipoli, surrounded by statues of angels and saints? What would it have been like when a family devoted a proportion of their produce to the poor and lived under the authority of local *caciques,* free of the two corrupting influences that came with the conquerors: drink and money?

What we have left in Santa María is the original square, with two original buildings fronting it, one converted into the museum to house our wealth of fine wooden statues of the saints. We have some of the original sites: the fount of fresh water, the little Calvary, and the church stands on the original foundations. We have the original music, but not of course any contemporary recordings. We have the original language of Guaraní, but not the original race. Some moved elsewhere in Paraguay when their protectors, the Jesuits, were expelled; others stayed and intermarried to give us our present *mestizo* (mixed) race. We can study and dream, but not flick back the hands of the clock to have a living experience.

There is no such thing as time travel, but to an extraordinary degree my dream was realised, when I went to visit the Jesuit reductions of Chiquitos in Bolivia. They are less famous than the Paraguayan reductions, partly because they were later copies of the Paraguayan model, and partly because they are so hard to reach, spread out over a vast area in the remote south east.

We hired a four-wheel-drive vehicle for eight days to go to Chiquitos. We crossed a terrifying bridge over the Río Grande, where the narrow planks were slippery with the swollen river water: a few days later two people were reported drowned in the flood. The first five hours were on asphalt, and then the road turned into compacted earth full of cracks and pits, and we drove for another five hours to reach the little church of Santa Ana, the least changed of any in the Chiquitos reductions.

The beautiful church faced us across a huge grassy square. With its simple pitched roof, painted façade, huge carved wooden columns supporting long colonnades, and separate bell tower, it was heart-rendingly beautiful, entirely typical of the reductions and quite different from any church not of that period. (Paraguay has a similar design in the church of Yaguarón, which was a Franciscan reduction rather than a Jesuit one, but of the same period: all the Paraguayan Jesuit churches have fallen down.) The bell tower is a wooden structure that stands apart, taller than the church and with steps winding up to the top – for ever linked in my mind with the Paraguayan Jesuit saint, Roque González, who was martyred with a blow to the head as he was fastening a bell to its thong in a new reduction at Caaró.

It was a hot sleepy day and the square seemed deserted. I circled the church, trying every door, until the back door to the sacristy swung open before me. The church was shuttered and dark, and I waited while my eyes began to adjust. Then a young man from the village walked in, and introduced himself as Francisco Rocha.

He threw open the shutters and doors and the light brought the church to life. He took me up to the choir loft, which every Jesuit church had over the entrance, and we gazed down the nave, towards the altar, towards the pulpit. The church has undergone minimal restoration, securing the structure but leaving everything possible from the past. The carved capitals were clearly visible from this height and so too were the wooden chandeliers, once holding candles and lowered by ropes. Until I came to Chiquitos I had not realised how dramatically different from today was the lighting in the churches, when angels and saints lined the walls, each holding a candle.

'In this chest,' said Francisco, showing me an old but very ordinary trunk, 'they found the music.' I was amazed. I had long ago read the story of how the hand-written music from the reductions – entirely lost in the Paraguayan destruction – was discovered as recently as 1972 in an old chest in a choir loft in Bolivia. So this was the chest. Since then there has been growing interest in Zipoli, who abandoned his musical career in Europe to bury himself among the South American indigenous.

'This is the only original organ left,' continued Francisco, showing me the wooden doors painted with flowers and plants. I knew all about how organs had been introduced into America by the Jesuit Anton Sepp (who had lived for a while in Santa María), and this one was made by Sepp's opposite number in Bolivia, P. Martin Schmid. Then Francisco opened the organ, and began to play. This was no museum piece, but a part of living, ongoing history. I was listening to a descendant of the original inhabitants playing the same music on the same organ in the same church, just as he did every week of the year, for the church of Santa Ana, like all the churches in Chiquitos, still functions as an active parish. I was inexpressibly moved.

The following morning I had another experience of the living past, at Mass in the church of San Miguel. The old tradition is maintained of a procession of the *caciques* (the indigenous leaders who were elected to run the political organisation of the reductions, for there were only two Jesuits in each town). They carried their traditional sticks of office, and sat in a carved bench against the left-hand wall of the church. At the consecration they did homage to the sacrament at the front of the centre aisle, and at the end of Mass they blessed the people who came to them. One of the *caciques* was a woman, and all were enormously welcoming to me, insisting that I go to drink *chicha* with them afterwards.

One special tradition in that Mass was the singing of the *anaustina* after communion, a Chiquitano hymn to the Blessed Sacrament. This was not Zipoli, and not baroque, but a repetitive rhythmic indigenous chant, to the accompaniment of a drum and a violin. I had thought the historic reductions were dead and I found they were alive. It was a resurrection moment.

(*First published 24 February 2007.*)

39

Lugo to Santa María

'Change is possible.' Fernando Lugo, resigned bishop and future presidential candidate in Paraguay, was speaking to a crowd in Santa María. He spoke quietly and reassuringly, and it sounded almost like a gospel invitation.

This was politics with a difference. Instead of the traditional political rant, he spoke gently. Instead of self-promotion, he devoted the first hour and a half of the meeting to listening to the concerns of the people, and only opened his mouth in the final ten minutes. Instead of the razzmatazz of pavilions, platforms and banners, he was seated in a simple circle of chairs under the trees. Instead of boasting about what he would do, he invited the people to become protagonists of their own future.

There was no party machine behind this visit. Lugo does not even have a party. The idea is that he should be the presidential candidate of the *Concertación* – a coming-together of all the opposition, from the Liberals to the Encuentristas, from the civil society groups working for change to the ordinary individuals who refuse to dabble in politics. Lugo even expects to get votes from many members of the ruling Colorado party, who joined the party on the principle of 'if you can't beat them, join them', but who know as well as anyone else does that the corrupt system is bad for the country.

Twenty minutes before he arrived, the dynamic young man who was buzzing around on his motor bike to coordinate the visit told me that Lugo would not after all be speaking on the local radio. 'The radio want to charge for it,' he said, 'and none of us have got any money.' I slipped the equivalent of a ten pound note into his hand and soon Lugo was on air.

Then Lugo came to our hotel and embraced me as an old friend. I took him into our simple wood and straw chapel and asked him to say a prayer. The disgraced bishop, suspended *a divinis* for going into politics, stood at the head of a little group of hotel staff, and gave thanks for the silence of the place, gazing at the Bible laid open on a hanging woven by the indigenous. Then he slipped off his sandals and walked over the woollen mats to touch the crucifix carved by the indigenous, and to turn and ask God's blessing on our work.

Lugo went next door to see the group of 35 craftswomen who do the appliqué embroidery for which Santa María is becoming known as a centre. Then Lugo and his group drove off to the Institute, as a place considered more politically neutral for his meeting than the town hall.

Once the people were invited to speak about their concerns for the country, the flow seemed unending. Corruption, *Coloradismo*, bandits in government, political fanaticism, fraud, bribery, unemployment, emigration … it all poured out, with increasing passion.

Lugo was regularly addressed as '*Monseñor*' – which reflects just how delicate is the situation. Is he a layman who once was a bishop? Not exactly. He may have asked for laicisation, but he remains a bishop not only in terms of the indelible character marked upon his soul but also in the hearts and the minds of those who support him. In any case, laicisation has been refused him, on the grounds that it is never – but never – granted to bishops.

This does not only mean that he is in Rome's bad books, but that he may not be able to stand at all, for the Paraguayan constitution declares that 'ministers of religion' cannot be presidential candidates. Lugo is technically 'a bishop without a ministry', in the words of the president of the Paraguayan Episcopal Conference. Does that make him a minister of religion, or not? It is a legal question that may have to be decided by the courts, and the courts are controlled to a large extent by the ruling party. If Lugo is blocked some people say it will spark an uprising comparable to that of the 1999 *Marzo Paraguayo* that overthrew the then president, Raúl Cubas.

Dressed in a yellow short-sleeved shirt and jeans, the bearded Lugo listened with his pen to the ready as the people of Santa María poured out their hearts. 'We have practically a perpetual dictatorship,' said a man called Gilberto, referring to the Colorados' 60-year rule. 'They are armed down to the tips of their toes, with the purchase of identity cards and their bribes of food and money. I beg you, *Monseñor*, to accept the candidatureship of the *Concertación*. There is no other candidate that can defeat them.'

At last Lugo rose to his feet. There was going to be a big international presence observing the 2008 election, he said. The campaign was indeed going to be 'very, very difficult. But not impossible.' And the way he said that 'not impossible' seemed to lift away all the anguish and the pain. Against the tricks of the government, Lugo continued, 'the Colorado party structure, the buying off of judges, fraud in the urns, bribes with money from the Yacyretá and Itaipú dams, from drug trafficking, from smuggling, and all of that, we have only one weapon: the conscience of the people. The process belongs to the people. The process has begun in the people. There is a possibility of change.'

And the people went home, inspired and hopeful, with *Jaikuaa Ikatuha* printed on their T-shirts: 'We know that it is possible.'

(*First published 28 April 2007.*)

40

Nicanor to Santa María

I wrote in my last column about the visit of Fernando Lugo, the resigned bishop who is trying to stand for President of Paraguay, but Santa María has also had a visit recently from the present President, Nicanor Duarte Frutos. He came to open a new housing estate of 40 homes for the poor.

We watched the helicopter fly in and land behind the *Poli Deportivo* (Sports Hall). Then Nicanor leapt into a jeep which whizzed him round and deposited him at the beginning of the welcoming line. He was wearing a brilliant red airtex shirt – the colour of his party, the Colorados ('the Coloureds'), who have been in uninterrupted power for 60 years. A recent newspaper ad spoke of 'our glorious Colorado party' with its 'brilliant civic spirit' to which the members pledge their 'fervour'.

Some of the crowd were fervent supporters of Coloradismo ('fanatical', say their critics). Others were residents of the new estate. All around people were wearing pro-Nicanor T-shirts, which said 'In a democracy competition is healthy. Yes to re-election.' The story behind this is that Nicanor has been trying to get the constitution changed so that he can stand for a second term of office. When the dictator Stroessner was ousted in 1989, the ban on re-election was introduced to stop another dictatorship developing. At the time of his visit, Nicanor was so desperate to stay in power that he had even been suggesting he might not call the 2008 election at all unless he could be a candidate.

When I saw one of my friends wearing the red-and-white T-shirt I said to her with surprise, 'I did not know you were a supporter of Nicanor.' 'I'm not,' she replied. 'I just wanted to have a new T-shirt.' Then I saw another friend with the T-shirt and the same exchange followed.

In double quick-time Nicanor had moved up the welcoming line, shaking hands, and found his way to the platform. Preliminary speeches were kept mercifully short so that Nicanor had time to tell of all the wonderful things he was doing for the poor. Strange that no one had associated him with doing wonderful things for the poor before. At smack-bang speed he greeted a veteran from the Chaco War, handed a symbolic key to one of the new residents, received a framed picture featuring his name, and embraced the stout woman who presented it – with her red lipstick matching the red hankie sticking out of her breast pocket. Then it was down from the stage, snip snip with the scissors through the tape in front of the first of the houses, into the house, out again, into the car, into the helicopter, and away. A couple more such visits in the Misiones region awaited his helicopter that morning. You have to admire the man's professionalism.

One of the new houses has gone to Isidro and Lida, who were my students at the Santa María Institute. The clever but desperately shy Lida is now studying English with us, while Isidro looks after the two children, and picks up occasional building work when he can. They have moved from one temporary place to another, from a borrowed house with no toilet, to a tiny office that just provided a roof over their heads, to a broken down place where the roof leaked. Now at last they have a solid and well-designed little house with a bedroom, kitchen/living room, bathroom, and space to build a second bedroom.

Leti and Nicolas and their baby qualified for another of the houses. Leti comes from a numerous family who are regular members of my Christian base community. I was godmother at their wedding – an event they spent six months saving up for, even though it was as simple as could be.

Gladys washes clothes to scrape a living, at 50 pence for a dozen items. A small bouncy woman with lots of energy, she previously lived in a tiny house without electricity where ten people squeezed into a couple of rooms. Now they have two houses they are only two and a half to a room.

Karina, my washerwoman, has another house. Her two children are some of the prettiest (though thinnest) children in Santa María. I know how needy the family is because Karina is always at my door asking for work first thing in the morning after I come back from a trip away, no matter how unexpected my return.

I rejoice that these deserving people have a decent home at last, and it is just a shame that there was so much delay over getting them finished. We were waiting for weeks for doors to be put on, then for paint to arrive. Without Nicanor's visit, we might still be waiting.

(*First published 30 June 2007.*)

41

Karina

I have lost my washerwoman, Karina. Only last month I was writing about her new house on the housing estate for low-income families, and now she has emigrated to Argentina, joining the constant dribble of Paraguayan young women emigrating in search of humble domestic work. Karina had an emotional motivation too – her husband had left her for another woman, and she had sisters already in Buenos Aires, one of whom she hoped could help with child-minding.

Some five years ago the dribble dried up, when Argentina went through an economic crisis so severe that the country ground to a halt. People could not withdraw their money from banks, those in work had their hours slashed to half time or less and desperate people were stealing wherever they could. The father of one of my students – who worked in a factory in Buenos Aires – went into a travel agent's to buy a bus ticket to Paraguay, only to be followed by a man with a gun who robbed him of all the money he had on him, so he could not travel. Such occurrences were commonplace, and the effect was deeply felt in Paraguay, as the money sent home to relatives dried up and Paraguayans in Buenos Aires began to return to their native land.

But the flight from Paraguay to Argentina is now back to its previous proportions, even though people are only earning something like a third of what they were earning before, in real terms. But something is always better than nothing, and for most people in Paraguay there is no work other than occasional odd jobs.

What propelled Karina into going to Argentina was another very typical Paraguayan situation: her husband went off with a younger woman. When Karina began working for me she was a slim and pretty young woman, but she is turning plump now, as happens to most of our women who start out as graceful nymphs. It is a question of nutrition, I suppose. The children, Jorgito ('little George') and Celeste ('Sky-blue'), are real beauties but with all the shyness that is characteristic of the poor. It is touching to see them faithfully trotting along hand in hand with their mother, not daring to leave her orbit for an instant. Her husband Jorge sells trinkets on the buses – hairbands, socks and mobile phone cases, strung up on a display board. He returns home with up to a couple of pounds a day, but Karina will never earn more than peanuts from washing clothes, for hardly anyone can afford to pay a laundry woman, even for the going rate of 40 pence a dozen items. (This is for washing by hand in cold water. Washing machines are very rare indeed.)

Karina's family do not come from Santa María, but from Encarnación – a city a couple of hours away. This means she will always be regarded as something of a stranger: 'She is not from here,' people say. So when Jorge left her (albeit with a legal but unenforceable agreement to support his children) she not only feared for being able to meet the household bills, but had no family support structure. 'Without my husband, there is nothing to keep me here,' she said.

Blinking back the tears, she asked me to send an urgent text message to her sister in Buenos Aires, giving the number of a friend's mobile phone where she could be rung back. Her sister rang and said she was out of work and could not send Karina the fare, but another sister in Buenos Aires was working and could help.

Paraguayans do not send money through the banks, because they do not have bank accounts. If they are sending money from further away, they use Western Union, which is rapid, easy to use and has innumerable branches – none in Santa María but several in neighbouring San Ignacio. But within the country – and probably from Argentina too – the usual method is by *encomienda*, which means sending a packet with the driver of a bus, not as a favour but as a paid service. This might sound more inconvenient than using the post and having something delivered to your door instead of to the bus terminal, but only a small minority use the post, so there has never been the bulk to make for an efficient service. Buses, by contrast, travel frequently, and there are several daily services from San Ignacio to Buenos Aires. So many people send parcels by *encomienda* that many bus companies have a separate office specifically devoted to sending and receiving parcels.

Surprisingly enough, it is safer to send money by *encomienda* than by post, as well as a lot faster. If you declare how much money you are sending and leave the envelope unsealed, the bus company is responsible for seeing that the amount you send is the amount that arrives. Some companies have even slimmed down the process so that the bank notes are not physically sent to their destination, but the amount paid in at one end is the amount that can be drawn out immediately at the other end.

And what is happening to Karina's nice new home on the estate? The going rate for renting a house is around £20 a month, and has not gone up in the seven years I have lived in Santa María. But few people can afford to pay that much – or even half that amount for a little house built for the poor – so Karina is looking for a solution sought by a number of others with empty properties, to 'lend' the house, that is, let people live in it rent-free. If you lend your house, then the occupier pays the electricity and water bill, and these utilities are kept active. But if you leave the house unoccupied and the electricity and water are cut off, there will be a fat fee for reconnection. Even to find people who can afford to meet these bills is not easy, so Karina went off to Argentina hopeful for the future, but leaving her house empty and its future unresolved.

(*First published 28 July 2007.*)

42

My new house

After seven years in Santa María de Fe, Paraguay, I have at last moved into my own house. It is a historic move for me personally, after living in rented accommodation for so long, but it also has implications for the wider community, because what I have built is in the style of the old Guaraní *casas de indios* from the time of the Jesuit reduction. It is the first such reconstruction to have been made in Paraguay, and will not be the last. Already a similar building is going up for the local sewing cooperative.

At last I have electrical points where I want them, instead of trailing electric flexes across the middle of my floor to squeeze eight or nine appliances off one single socket. At last I have full-length mirrors, instead of half-length mirrors in the inside doors of wardrobes. At last I have a back garden that is closed off so that I can leave my hammock out at night without fear that it will be pinched. At last I have my own pottery dishes, that give me joy each time I use them, instead of borrowed pyrex non-matching plates. At last I have beautiful wood and leather furniture from the Pa'i Pukú school for children from poor families in the Chaco, instead of metal armchairs with brightly coloured plastic seating.

But what is the greatest joy is to see how much the local people like the new-old house. The temptation for *campesinos* struggling to edge out of poverty is to build a town house in the country and undervalue the traditional architecture. It would not have occurred to them to build a house such as existed 300 years ago, in adobe, with a roof of bamboo covered with mud and then with porous clay tiles, and a long veranda supported on big wooden pillars of *lapacho* hardwood. But now they have seen it, they adore it and I am told a dozen times a day how lovely my house is.

We took the model from the museum, which is an original building from the reduction, and copied the methods of construction and all the dimensions and materials. The walls are 70cm thick. The doors are massive and panelled. The roof is high with open beams, and wide porticos run the full length of the building front and back. In the reduction, these porticos were the public pavements, and the long houses ran in continuous rows along each side of the central square and behind it in parallel lines.

What is different about my house is that, unlike the original *casas de indios,* it has a kitchen and a bathroom (though they are built so as to be invisible from outside), that it has eight windows and two doors (whereas the museum has twelve doors and only three windows), and that I have all to myself the space that would previously have been occupied by three or four families. (Each Guaraní family had a square room to themselves, with an external door to the front and to the back, and often no window because the open doors served to let in the light.) It is almost like living in a cathedral, with the high ceiling towering above me and one big living room encompassing a dining area, a sitting area and a study area.

When I first came here to share the life of the poor I would have been horrified if I had known that I would end up living in such luxury. But I reached the conclusion that I can do more for the poor by employing them to construct the kind of building that Santa María needs but cannot afford, than by sitting on my money and pretending I have not got it.

My building (at £30,000) has worked out more expensive than the next *casa de indios* will be, because mine has been the first and I am paying for a certain amount of experiment. We have taught local people the techniques for making adobe blocks – a technique long since forgotten – but now they will be able to build their own houses for minimal cost with the earth that is free beneath their feet and the labour that they can provide themselves. We have restored the technique of using bamboo for ceilings, which is still to be found in some of the oldest houses but was no longer used by builders. We opened a small tile-making factory in the countryside, where with the help of donkeys and primitive technology the techniques of tile-making were rediscovered after a break of some 30 years. We have established the practice that for every *lapacho* tree felled, ten more must be planted.

One technical issue still to be resolved is on the constitution of the plaster on the adobe walls. The current mixture is 45 per cent Paraguay's local red earth, 45 per cent washed sand, and 10 per cent cement, a blend which Paraguayan architects have used successfully in smaller adobe buildings elsewhere in the country. But it is cracking already, and the suggestions received so far include mixing in straw, cow dung, lime, or honey, adding more sand and omitting the cement.

In Genesis, Jacob worked seven years in a foreign land in the attempt to win Rachel as his bride – the same period I have been living in Paraguay. Now I have gone to all this trouble and expense, I had better be another seven years in Paraguay to make it worthwhile.

(*First published 3 November 2007.*)

43

Moxos choir

In the film *The Mission* – which is the story of where I live – nothing is more moving than the music, and no moments of the music more moving than when the indigenous sing. The *Ave María,* sung by a chorus of children as a foreign visitor enters the church, tears at the heart strings. So too does the solo by the young semi-naked boy, standing on a pedestal in front of the slave-dealers who didn't believe he had a soul. This sound is neither European nor indigenous, but a potently creative mix of the two.

At the time the film was made, the authentic scores from the Jesuit-Guaraní reductions had not yet been found, but Ennio Moricone did a great job of inventing a sound that was European in its composition style but indigenous in its performance style. Since then, the old wooden chest in the organ loft of Santa Ana, Chiquitos, has been opened, and the riches of Domenico Zipoli and other composers (both European and indigenous) found inside. This is the music that was once sung in Santa María de Fe and the other Paraguayan reductions, but was lost or destroyed after the 1768 Expulsion of the Jesuits. The Bolivians in Chiquitos originally received their music from Paraguay, and can now give it back to us.

Zipoli was an Italian Jesuit of the generation of Vivaldi, who gave up a potentially brilliant musical career in Rome to bury himself for the rest of his life in the South American missions. The Guaraní loved music so much that they would creep out of the forests to the river banks, when Jesuits playing music were drifting downstream. Under the Jesuits they learned not only to sing and play, but also to make instruments and to compose. The Tyrolese Jesuit, Anton Sepp, who lived in my town of Santa María de Fe, wrote that his little choir of eight young boys sing the *Laudate Pueri* 'with such poise, such grace and style, that in Europe it would hardly be believed, from these poor, naked, innocent little Indian children'. Sepp was the first person in this continent to build an organ, and he is also known as the father of the Paraguayan harp.

Here in Paraguay new CDs of Zipoli are issued almost every year. The conductor and the singers are Paraguayan, but they are middle-class people from Asunción and the music sounds like something recorded in Europe. What we have lacked up till now is the vigorously different sound that would have come out of the indigenous choirs, just as the Guaraní copies of European statues – though copies – have a flavour that no European can ever imitate.

On the last Saturday of October, that sound came back to Misiones, Paraguay, sung by a young indigenous choir from San Ignacio de Moxos, Bolivia, which was a Jesuit reduction based on the Paraguayan model. Moxos is another place where original sheets of music were found. If these young people looked about 14, that was because they *were* about 14 – between 14 and 23, to be exact. They came from several different native peoples, their dark skin beautifully emphasised by their loose, sleeveless robes of unbleached cotton edged with coloured braid. The boys wore bead necklaces and the girls had white beads woven into their short black plaits. The highly professional conductor, Raquel Maldonado, is only 29 years old, but has already led her choir to over 100 concerts in seven countries.

The sound was stunning, with an energy and a purity that was breathtaking. All the singers were versatile musicians, playing at least one instrument, and moving effortlessly from violin to recorder to handbeaten drum, and even to a little whistle shaped like a bird that gave out a bird song. When they played the violin they practically danced around the sanctuary with it. When they played the recorder, there was a poignancy reminiscent of Father Gabriel's oboe solo at the opening of *The Mission*.

They sang in Guaraní, in Spanish and in Latin, and the final piece began with a candelit, penitential procession for Holy Week. The music became quieter and quieter, until there was just one voice and one drum: then the candle was blown out. Shortly afterwards there was an explosion of light and sound from the back of the church, and the choir danced up the aisle in simply enormous feather headdresses, with brilliantly coloured plumes of blue, white and red. This is how they celebrate Easter morning in Moxos.

Stunned, as much as the rest of the audience, most of whom had never been to a concert before in their lives, I bought five copies of their CD *Tras las Huellas de la Loma Santa*, and wished afterwards I had bought 50.

(*First published 1 December 2007.*)

CRCR   SDSD

On the next visit of the Moxos choir to Paraguay, I did indeed buy 50 CDs, for selling in the Santa María Hotel.

44

Land invasion

The English class this week was all about protests: animal testing, star wars, equal pay and multinational companies. But one of the students was absent: Luis was taking part in a protest himself. It was a land occupation – one of 19 simultaneous invasions around Paraguay by landless peasants that took place at 4.00 pm on 14 June. Discussion of Luis' protest gave the lesson what is called in English-teaching jargon 'authenticity'.

Six days later he came to my house in the evening, after the most bitterly cold week Paraguay has had this year. He wanted to tell me about the occupation, but his fellow demonstrators were afraid of the press, so he had to talk to me off the site. There were 250 people in the occupation, he said, including many mothers and children and elderly people, and they were hungry. He had been asked to look for food. They could find enough firewood on the land to cook, but nothing to put in the pots other than the mandioc root. They were sleeping in tents made of black plastic sheeting and some of the poorest had no blankets. Children were clinging to their parents, as the temperature fell to 3 degrees. The only way to sleep was to light a fire, huddle around it to warm up, and catch a couple of hours' sleep before the cold woke you up again.

Why were they were doing it? That was easy to answer – because they had no land, and wanted to be able to grow enough crops to live in dignity. But why were they doing it *now*? Partly because they had not expected the weather to turn so cold, and partly because they had not expected the invasion to be so successful. Usually an invasion is dislodged within 48 hours, making a point that may yield some future fruit. But in this case, they had been there a full week without being thrown out, and were convinced that the delay was because the land actually had no legal owner.

There is supposedly an owner of the 4,000 hectares that they are occupying (though in fact they are only occupying a small enclosed area of it next to the road, where they can protect themselves with watchmen). But the paperwork this alleged owner is presenting is contradictory and does not add up. He does not use any of the land himself, but over the years has been earning an income from renting just a small part of it to Brazilians, who are planting genetically modified soya. One thing Paraguayans are certain of is that they regard genetically modified crops as a threat to health, and another thing they are certain of is that they resent better-off Brazilians taking their land off them because they can pay more.

Luis was upbeat and confident. 'We are very united,' he said, 'with a lot of hope and a lot of faith.' A strict discipline operates in the occupation: regular duties as sentinels, sharing all food in common, and no alcohol. There is no squabbling. Every morning at 7.00 am there is a roll call: those who are absent will go down in the list when the time comes to allot parcels of land to the victors. 'We know our objectives and are determined to see things through to the end,' he said. 'Our hope grows day by day.'

I began to prepare a hot soup for Luis but he turned it down in favour of warming his insides with *caña* (a sugar-cane spirit like rum). He did not expect to get another drink for a week. 'This land has no owner,' he repeated, '*esta tierra no tiene dueño*', and I was reminded of the slogan of the great Guaraní leader Sepe, who said exactly the opposite when the Spaniards tried to give his people's land to the Portuguese as part of the 1750 Treaty of Madrid. '*Esta terra tem dono*,' Sepe proclaimed (in Portuguese): 'This land has an owner.' He was killed in the war of resistance, but the Guaraní today regard him as a saint.

In between the different villages in the countryside, said Luis, there are thousands of hectares of land and nobody knows who they belong to.

There are people who do not even know how much land they have, while others live in misery because they have none.

Luis is one of nine leaders who have been warned that their arrest is imminent. It is a risk that he has taken not so much for himself – for he has other plans for his future – but out of solidarity with the poorest in Santa María, to help them struggle for their cause. 'They work like mules,' he told me, 'and they live in misery.' That is, if they are lucky enough to find work.

'It's sad,' he said, 'because I am missing my English classes. But what is sadder still is to see how people in my village are suffering.'

(*Written 21 June 2008, but first published 25 July 2009.*)

45

Mural

When disaster strikes, there is a natural tendency to look for a crumb of comfort: 'It could have been worse, at least x didn't happen.' But when Nino Sotelo and I gazed this morning at what had happened to the mural he was painting on my wall, we echoed to each other, 'This could not be more serious.' The plaster was coming loose and in a couple of places was about to fall off the wall.

How could this have happened again? In my earlier piece (see p.129) I recounted how the plaster fell off my adobe wall the first time. I used to hear it thump down in great clumps in the night, leaving a dusty mess over everything. A great deal of research went on before the replastering, and I translated for Pedro, the designer of my house (technically not quite an architect, as he had not had the money to finish his architecture studies), many contributions from the English-speaking world, with email advice coming in from Colombia, Chile, Mexico, California, Zaire, Cameroon and Kisumu.

A lot of the advice was contradictory, some saying you must use cement, if only a little, to give strength, others that you never should or it will crack; some saying you must use straw or other fibres such as rice husks to hold the plaster together, others saying that the lime will consume any organic material and leave holes; some saying you should use a metal mesh to keep the plaster on the wall, others saying that the nails needed to peg on the mesh would rust; some saying that the adobe must be completely dry before plastering, others that you must wet it to make the plaster stick. Pedro was eager to get on with the replastering – at his own expense – to restore the look of the embarrassingly blemished building, but I insisted on a trial area first – on the back wall. We waited a month, the experiment appeared to have been successful, and I allowed the internal replastering to go ahead.

One of my inside walls is huge and has no windows: it is the wall that backs on to what would be the next dwelling, if there was one. I thought it would be wonderful to invite one of Paraguay's best artists, Nino Sotelo, to paint a big mural here of the Jesuit history of Santa María de Fe. Nino is best known for the huge murals lining the stairwell up to the tower in the Basilica of Caacupe, telling how the Virgin of Caacupe was carved by an indigenous man as thanksgiving for deliverance from enemies. I sought out the artist's name and phone number, persuaded him to come down to Santa María, and he agreed to undertake the commission.

The work would take ten days to a fortnight, Nino said, and he began on 12 January. In fact, six weeks later the work was still unfinished, despite the fact that Nino sleeps in the house and works until 11 o'clock each night. Seeing it take form has been an amazing experience, and we have worked together closely on the historical data that would enter the picture. Day after day more people have come to the house to gaze at the great art work, with gasps of wonder. The drama, the colours, the mood of struggle and devotion, of fears and joys, and the sheer size of the work at 30 square metres – all go to make this an important art work that, we believed, would bring many people to visit Santa María.

At the top we see the famous Jesuit, Antonio Montoya – the illegitimate son of a Peruvian indigenous mother – blessing three Belgian priests as he sends them to found new reductions in Itatín, now north of the Paraguayan border. One of these three fair-skinned Jesuits is the great Jacques Ransonnier, who was to name one of the new missions Nuestra Señora de Fe, after the Belgian devotion to Notre Dame de Foy. Ransonnier was a man of immense energy and austerity, who wore his health out in a few years and on his death bed asked forgiveness of his body for the ill-treatment he had inflicted on it. In the mural we see him walking barefoot in his patched and faded soutane, carrying the small model of the Belgian statue beside the Guaraní caciques, as together they lead their people in an exodus from a burnt and smouldering village, attacked by the slave-traders from São Paulo.

The lower part of the mural shows the square in the new site – the square just outside my window. We worked hard on the historical data for the form of the original church, the bell tower, the cemetery to one side and the school and workshops to the other. Several times Nino had to repaint details, until we were satisfied that they were accurate to the best of our knowledge. The great statue of St Mary of Faith is being carried out of the door of the church on the patronal feast day. And one night Nino painted into the crowd his faithful assistant, Ismael – a 17-year-old boy with musical and artistic leanings, from a local poor family, who has been with Nino throughout his time here, fetching and carrying paints to him as he sat high up on his scaffolding.

But when Nino got up the morning after painting Ismael into the mural, he found to his horror that the plaster was beginning to lose its key and bulge out of the wall. It was the beginning of the end. 'What is the point of continuing? There is no point,' said Nino.

It has been a day of deep depression. Pedro is four hours' drive away, attending to his wife in hospital after a caesarian, but the joy of the birth has been overshadowed by the news from Santa María. The building foreman arrived this afternoon and offered his resignation: 'What has happened pains me to my soul,' he said. Nino remarkably kept smiling, but only because, he said, 'It is the only way to keep the tears away.'

After a day of sitting in the square, uncertain what to do, Nino Sotelo decided to continue and finish his work, even though he knew it would fall down. Before it all fell down, we rescued six sections of the mural (1m x 80cm) in broken pieces, to form mosaic-like framed pictures. Nino also repainted onto canvas three larger sections, and was going to paint three more, but died before he could do so. For the continuation of the story of my house, see the Afterword (p.184).

(*First published 29 March 2008.*)

46

Election

Here in Paraguay we are over-stimulated and exhausted all at the same time, but very, very happy. All the week leading up to the Paraguayan election of 20 April I was restless: all the opinion polls showed Fernando Lugo in the lead, but there was little confidence in the country that he could actually beat the ruling Colorado party machine with its last-minute tricks. People I asked all thought Lugo would be the true winner but the Colorados would wrest victory from him either by fraud or by refusing to hand over power.

The Colorado advertising in the papers was terrific in mood but empty in content. Against the ex-bishop Lugo they said: 'The Pope doesn't accept him. Don't you accept him. Don't vote for him.' In favour of their own party they showed crowds of people riding on horseback and waving red flags: 'The red trumpet call sounds out all over the country ...The Colorado party is the red blood that makes our soil fertile with generosity and heroism, so that Paraguay can be born again. It is the flag that waves in the trenches of liberty. It's the hoarse cry that wakes in the throat of the *campesino* in the morning. It's the *urundeý* tree that resists the onslaught of the winds. It's the fertile earth where revolutionary ideas of redemption and social justice germinate. All this is the Colorado Party. That is why we are going to win on 20 April.' Great advertising, but what did it add up to? Nothing.

Last Sunday I rose early for the 6.00 am start of voting in Paraguay, and rushed over to the polling station at the primary school. My job was to take photos of Colorado members hanging around to press money into people's palms to buy their vote. Piti, the woman who collects my rubbish, was delegated to tell me who to photograph. 'That big man in the anorak,' she said. I know his name – he's a neighbour of mine – but I won't embarrass him by recording it.

He saw me with my camera and made a face: 'So the BBC is here!' he said. I heard him explaining to colleagues that he could not do anything because he was being filmed, and he kept on shooting looks in my direction to see if I was still there. The legal penalty for vote-buying is a prison sentence, but no one ever gets charged.

Lots of vehicles were arriving, all with Colorado stickers, bringing the poorest in to vote from the countryside, most of whom had been bribed with either money or food. They come to expect this little payment, come election time.

It did indeed seem incredible that Lugo could win against this organisation. The Colorados have money so they have fleets of cars. The Alliance supporting Lugo had very little money but had managed to hire one lorry for each *compañía,* so if Lugo supporters were committed enough to wait around for it they could get transport in.

Then the BBC did indeed ring me. I now had two tasks to do: photograph the bribes and collect *vox pops.* Piti tipped me off again: 'He is going to give some money to that man,' and I rushed up with my camera just as he was fishing a handful of notes from his pocket. His colleagues suddenly warned him I was there and he pushed them back into his pocket. 'Look,' he said, 'I respect what you do in Santa María, but just leave us in peace, will you?'

A while later a car drove up and two men got out to talk to the big man, and Piti told me to be ready with my camera again. The group stood around in a circle looking bothered, waiting to do something when I would go away, but I wouldn't. I really did not know what they were up to until they gave up and drove off and Piti told me: 'They were the people bringing more money.'

I asked the big man if I could record an interview with him. He agreed readily. 'What do you think of Lugo?' I asked him. 'He has very strong links with terrorists and with kidnappers,' he said, 'he is unfaithful to the

Catholic Church and does not respect the laws of the Vatican, and he has nil knowledge of how to manage an administration.'

A spy told us that the Colorados were planning a power cut during the count so they could steal some ballot boxes under cover of dark. I went to the Santa María Hotel to borrow an emergency light, which comes on automatically as soon as the power goes, and left it with a member of the Lugo Alliance inside the polling station. At 4.00 pm the polls closed. Three districts in Asunción did indeed have power cuts, but we escaped it in Santa María.

At 5.05 pm a neighbour ran up to my house and told me the first two exit polls had given Lugo a 6 per cent lead. (When the official result came a few hours later the figures were even more dramatic: Lugo had won with a 10 per cent margin.) Soon people were seizing guitars and dancing in the streets. Boys on motorbikes sped round the square for joy and fireworks were let off. We saw Lugo on television saying that 'the little ones' too are capable of victory, and that his would be 'a humble and a modest presidency'. Then a *caravana* started spontaneously.

Usually a *caravana* is a Colorado display of force, with endless lines of cars peeping their horns: the Colorados pay £20 to the driver and another £20 for the petrol. But this one was a *caravana* of the poor, and it was made up of people on foot, dancing for joy and waving their arms and singing to the music of the Lugo campaign song, with wild enthusiasm. I'll never forget María Dolores, one of the quietest and most diffident of all our students, singing her heart out and throwing her arms in the air in wild abandon, along with everyone else.

Into the early hours of the morning the *caravana* went out into the countryside, and in hamlet after hamlet the people poured out of their homes to follow it, crying 'Lugo! Lugo!' The next day a number of people had literally lost their voices.

All around me people were turning out to be ecstatic Lugo supporters, though I had never discussed politics with them before: my builder, the man who brings my newspaper, a woman who does *ao po'i* embroidery, the man in the corner shop, the man who makes wrought-iron window bars, a receptionist from the Santa María Hotel. When someone came to my door there would be a split-second pause, and then they would say 'At last!' and we would both beam and embrace.

When I passed people in the street – known or unknown – they would greet me with 'Congratulations!' or 'At last!' or 'Victory!' or 'Lugo! Lugo!' The most amazing thing was how many of the most enthusiastic were Colorado members, wanting the *cambio* – the change. It was even evident that many people who had felt pressured into working for the Colorado campaign had actually cast their votes for Lugo. 'This is not the victory of any party,' they said, 'this is the victory of the people.'

(*First published 10 May 2008.*)

47

How women have suffered

Earlier this year a woman called Griselda returned to visit Santa María, after she fled from here 50 years ago. This is her story.

Griselda grew up poor and underprivileged. She was illiterate, and she did not have an identity card or even a birth certificate. Such people are the marginalised of the marginalised. As far as the government knows, they do not exist.

But when she reached her early teens Griselda got a boyfriend. A girl was born, Lorena, and a year later a little boy, Nico. Before long the boyfriend began to be violent towards Griselda. He dragged her along the ground by her hair, when he suspected she was going with another man. He threatened that if she left him he would find her and kill her.

So when Griselda could not bear it any more she did not say where she was going. She just disappeared, leaving her children behind her. She was only 17 years old.

Lorena, who was now three years old, was brought up by Griselda's sister, and little Nico by his grandmother. As the months and then years went by there was still no word from Griselda. She was safe from her partner's reprisals, but at what a cost!

When Lorena and Nico grew up they were determined to find their mother. They tried to place notices in newspapers and have Griselda mentioned on television. But no one would accept their appeals because there were no documents to show who she was. Griselda's sister would sometimes wake up crying out, 'My sister is surely dead'.

Fifty years passed. Lorena went to work as a domestic in Buenos Aires, and Nico found work in the east of Paraguay. Then one day earlier this year, when Lorena was back in Santa María on her holiday, a friend turned up with a phone number. The friend was working in the regional government offices, and one of her colleagues had told her that – by an extraordinary coincidence – her husband was Griselda's nephew.

Full of trepidation, Lorena rang the number in Asunción and spoke to the nephew. He took the phone round to Griselda and she took the call, seated in front of her new partner and their three children.

'Is that Griselda?' asked Lorena.

'Yes,' she said.

'Then you're my mum.'

'You're making a mistake. I didn't have any children before I came to Asunción.'

Lorena insisted, 'Yes you are, you're my mum.'

Griselda denied it again. But when she had hung up, she cried, and she cried, and she cried. And then her family knew that she must have been living a lie for all those years and that she was weeping for her children.

The nephew took the phone again and sought out the Calls Received register. He rang Lorena straight back. 'She *is* your mum,' he said, 'You must come and see her. I'll meet you at the bus terminal.' When Lorena saw her mother she almost fainted, because Griselda looked just like her, only 14 years older.

Shortly after this reunion, Griselda came back to Santa María, for the first time in 50 years, to meet her other relatives. She told her story, slowly, bit by bit, because the tears would not stop coming.

When she had run away, all those years ago, she had gone to Asunción to look for work. She got a job with a naval officer, who expected from his pretty young maid the usual favours. When the wife realised what was happening, she trumped up a charge to get Griselda arrested. This was in the days of Stroessner's dictatorship, when female prisoners were regularly dumped in the River Paraguay with stones round their waists. To prevent Griselda being killed, another employee of the naval officer, called Nestor, bribed the police to get her out of jail.

The two became lovers, and had three children. But Griselda never let on that she had had a former family. Over the years, life became hard in this marriage too: Nestor went through a period of heavy drinking, and Griselda had to work, washing clothes, to bring up the children.

No one knew Griselda's secret. But they all wondered why she would always weep at the family feasts of Christmas and New Year. Her children would ask her, 'Where are our grandparents? Why don't we ever see them?' And Griselda would cry and say nothing. The more time went by, the more impossible it became to admit to having told a lie for so many years. She could only grieve for the secret family in her heart.

One of Griselda's relatives in Santa María came to me with the story and asked me to write it up. 'I want people to know,' she said, 'how much women have suffered here in Paraguay.'

(*First published 25 October 2008.*)

ଓଋ   ຊ໐ຊໍ

Names have been changed.

48

Born in poverty

Jesus was born in poverty. The little baby with his soft skin, barely perceptible breaths and tightly clenched fists was settled down to sleep in a manger filled with straw, while angels sang in the starlight. It is all very romantic. But what is it really like when babies are born in poverty?

A constant problem is paying for the birth. We are lucky in Misiones to have an 'SOS Children's Villages' hospital (the *Aldea*), but even their nominal fees are hard for the poor to meet. You are not discharged until you have paid the bill, and often the new fathers, who should be radiant with pride and joy, instead are sick with worry because they do not know how to pay to get their wife and child home.

Then there is the problem of getting to the hospital. There are few buses that leave from Santa María, so if you miss (for example) the 1.00 pm bus you will have to wait until 4.30 pm before there is another. Last time I went for, and missed, the 1.00 pm bus there were a couple of other women at the bus stop who had also missed it – an enormously pregnant, very young, shy girl, with a friend. They were going to the *Aldea* because the baby was already on the way. I rang for a taxi, but if I had not been travelling, what would they have done?

Many newborn babies have health problems. Little Megali was brought to visit me in my house by her mother and grandmother, apparently quite well, but only a few days later we heard she had a hole in her heart. There was a great deal of desperate scraping around for money before an overseas donation of £200 secured the operation that she needed. Without it she would have died.

Not all the babies born here are so lucky. One of my students became pregnant by a boy at the sugar factory where she had done her work placement, but she denied outright that she was expecting, and squeezed her tummy into tight clothes. In the end the bump could not be hidden any longer, and she looked like a huge, round ball, being a tiny girl herself. The baby was born with water on the brain, and then the mother did everything possible to save the child that she had not wanted. There were community activities to raise funds, and the Cuban doctor who was posted to Santa María at the time could not believe that the state would not pay for the operation, as it would in her country. After a long delay the baby was operated on, but she died a few weeks later.

Blanca's baby died much more quickly. Blanca was another unmarried mother, but she had a steady boyfriend, Diego. She went to all her antenatal check-ups, and nothing went wrong until she went into labour two weeks early with the baby in breech position. There was a delay as the doctors disagreed about whether to operate or not, and the baby swallowed the amniotic fluid, which affected his internal organs. There was a shortage first of incubators, then of intensive care facilities, and finally of medicines. Santiago died at only two days old, and I heard about the death before I had even heard about the birth. My keen memories of the funeral were of the red-faced sobs of Diego's brother, and of Blanca's childlike profile as she streamed silent tears, with her mother and father on either side of her. It was agonising to see this young girl bear the full weight of a mother's grief, as she gave the coffin one final kiss.

The first baby born to my friends Leti and Nicolas was born in 2005 and was healthy. I have photos of the happy parents with baby, in their poor little dark hut with a dirt floor, plastic sheeting hanging down one wall and a picture of St Joseph on the bare bricks behind them. It was not so dissimilar from the Bethlehem stable. Two years later they had another child, but this time Leti became infected and was so sick she nearly died. She was several weeks with her baby in a far-off hospital, and they had to remove her womb. Yet she came home more buoyed up with the love of her new daughter than with the depression that she could have no more children.

A baby is always a miracle, but never more so than when a child is born in poverty. For that reason, Leti called her daughter Milagro, which means miracle. And for that reason, the angels in Bethlehem must have sung all the louder, and the star shone all the brighter.

(*First published 3 January 2009.*)

ославов   வ

The Aldea maternity hospital has closed down in Misiones for lack of funding. It is a local tragedy.

Blanca's photo appears on the cover of this book.

49

Mother of 20

Nidia Vencelada Jiménez Benítez is the mother of 20 children. I went out to interview her at her simple house at Cerro Costa – one of the *compañías* or hamlets in the municipal area of Santa María de Fe – and found a small, plump woman with wiry features and a great sense of humour.

She invited me to sit down in the shade in front of her house, together with my taxi driver and a student from the Santa María Institute who was making the introduction. She was accompanied by one of her grown-up daughters, Arsenia, and her husband Modesto, a serious, white-haired man who sat to the side. He fed in the accurate details, while Nidia gave the spice to the conversation, her face sharp as a bird's, her grey hair drawn back.

We exchanged gifts: I gave her exercise books for her grandchildren, and she gave me bananas from her garden. I asked Nidia how old she was. She said she was 65, but Modesto corrected her to 66. She has lived all her life in Cerro Costa, where her first nine children were fathered by a local man, Eduviji, who died two years ago. The remaining 11 are children of Modesto.

So how did it all begin? Nidia was 15 when she had her first child, Tolentino de Jesús, in 1956. She gave birth with a local midwife, with great joy, and took no painkillers, neither for this birth nor for any other.

The baby was healthy, and so was she. Every evening she prays, asking for good health, knowing how fundamental that is. Tolentino never married, and he died from a heart attack last year in Buenos Aires, where he was working as a building labourer.

Who was her second child? Nidia had to ask Modesto. 'Gregoria,' he told her. Gregoria still lives in Cerro Costa, and has four children herself. 'How many grandchildren have you got?' I asked. 'Oh, I can't count them, there are lots of them,' she said, as though I had asked a stupid question. 'Not to mention great grandchildren.' At the end of our conversation I totted up just the grandchildren she had told me about, and got to 54.

The third (she was prompted by Modesto) was Eduardo, who also went to Argentina to work as a builder. They came in the sequence boy, girl, boy, girl, and they came every year, explained Nidia. When we got to the end of the sequence and worked it out, we modified this arithmetic to one every 18 months, since she had had 20 between the ages of 15 and 45. 'You see,' she said, 'there didn't used to be any remedy that would stop you having children. Like there didn't used to be television either.' Did she have television now? 'Yes, we got one five years ago.'

The fourth was Fermina, who went to Argentina to work in domestic service. Next was Gerónimo, and he went to work in the Alto Paraná region of Paraguay, which had more agricultural work because it was under-populated. And so it continued, with Cristina coming sixth, who now had four children of her own and lived just down the road. The children can all go to school in Cerro Costa now, for all the grades except the top two classes of secondary school, but Nidia and all her children had to go to school in Santa María, and mostly they went on horseback.

'Who came next?', Nidia asked her husband, again and again. Now the boy-girl-boy rule was broken. Dionisia was the seventh, and she also went to Alto Paraná. Eighth was Mariano, who has eight children himself. Next came another boy, Victoriano, but he only lived for three days. Nidia did not know why he died, but he became ill very suddenly one evening, and died very quickly. In those days not even Santa María had a health centre. You would have to carry a sick child as far as San Ignacio, nearly three hours' journey away on foot, but less on horseback.

We had now reached 1968, the year when she began to live with Modesto, though they got married later on. Their first child, Primitiva, went to work as a domestic servant in another part of Paraguay, and has eight children of her own. So far we have got to ten children – only halfway through.

Three more boys followed: Nicolás, who works on the land in Cerro Costa; Martín, who works as a builder in Argentina; and Marcelino who works on the land in Alto Paraná. The fourteenth child was Aurelia, who lives in the next hamlet, then another boy, Dionisio, and three girls in a row: Crispina, Pabla and Modesta, who all live in their home village, and have five children between them and one on the way. While we are talking, a barefoot 7-year-old boy wanders past – son of Crispina.

Miguel, the nineteenth, lives close to Aurelia. Which leaves … Arsenia! At 21 years old, Arsenia is not a little one any more, but she is the only one who still lives in the parental home. She was also the only one to be born in a clinic, instead of at home with a community midwife. Nidia herself has acted as community midwife to one of her daughters-in-law, delivering Dionisio's child.

So what was it like to have such a big family? Arsenia likes it a lot. Christmas is always a fun time, with hoards of family swarming round, but they never have all the family together at once: it just would not be possible in their small space.

What was the worst thing about having a big family? Nidia had no hesitations: 'When they die. When a child dies it is the mother who suffers most.' She has seen two of her children die: Victoriano at three days, and her first child, Tolentino, last year. Nidia had to raise the funds to go to Buenos Aires to bring the body home, which she did by selling two oxen.

They have managed to replace the oxen, and their other animals comprise a cow, two pigs, two turkeys, three dogs, one cat, one parrot and 15 hens. They eat chicken once a week. When they are better off, they get a second cow.

Nidia gets up at 5.00 am every morning to work in the fields. By 9.00 am she is back home, for fear of staying too long in the bright sun. She drinks mate, and receives visits from her children. They take their products in an ox cart to sell in Santa María and the nearby towns: water melons, mandioc, oranges and grapefruit, sweet potatoes and beans. They even sell firewood.

The family have known three houses: their first one was by the slope of the hill and just had one room with two beds in it and an outside latrine, and no land. They upgraded to a house with three rooms and five beds, and three hectares of land: most of the family were born and lived there, squashing into the available beds. Their current house still has three rooms, but it has ten hectares.

Is 20 children a record? Nidia does not know of anyone with more. One thing is certain: with the advent of TV and all that, mothers of 20 children are a dying breed.

(*First published 7 March 2009.*)

ଔଔ   ৪০৪০

Tablet *reader Francis Pimentel Pinto wrote in to say that 'the wife of my mother's deceased brother had 27 children!'*

50

Motorbikes

One of the biggest changes I have seen in Santa María over the last couple of years is a growth in the number of motorbikes. It is a sign that we are now a developing country rather than a country sinking ever deeper into poverty and stagnation, which is what I experienced in my early years here. So motorbikes are a good thing, are they? Well, I don't know. In a country with the appalling levels of road safety that Paraguay has, the growth of motorbikes is accompanied by a terrifying rise in mortality levels. It is hard to call that 'development'.

We are living in a country where no one needs to take a driving test, not even to drive a car, let alone to ride a motorbike. You get a licence to drive a car simply by going to the town hall and paying a fee, as though it were a dog licence. Drink driving is against the law, but you will not be breathalysed unless you have actually caused an accident, and there is no community consciousness about the immorality of it. As for wearing crash helmets on motorbikes, the law in Paraguay is not enforced. In Lugo's Paraguay there are more police checks than there were before, but establishing a law-abiding society will be a long, slow haul.

One day last July I heard a motorbike pass my house and then a fearful screeching sound. When I looked out there was a young man prone on the ground and pools of blood leading to where he had been thrown. The young man, Dani, had collided at the corner with a car. Neither driver had looked before charging across the intersection, but, with no driving test, neither driver had been taught that you should look. Dani was one of the lucky ones: he broke his leg so badly that it is still healing in plaster today but his head, though unprotected, was not hit.

Not so lucky poor Richard, who crashed the new motorbike he got for his birthday and is severely brain damaged and in a wheelchair. Nor was Jaime so lucky: he too was brain damaged in a motorbike crash, but died within a couple of weeks. He had been riding on the back and the driver had been drinking. I went to the wake. Drink was also a factor in a motorbike crash only a few days later, just one block from my house, when both driver and passenger were killed.

It is hard to understand why the penny does not drop that no one should go on a motorbike without a crash helmet, and that no one should drive when under the influence of alcohol. But every time there is an accident it is regarded as just bad luck. People still ride two, three, or even four to a motorbike, with babies and little children dangling on so that the family can all journey together. It never occurs to anyone that this is dangerous. As many as 17 per cent of those killed in traffic accidents are babies and children under 14.

Just after New Year there was a motorbike accident when three young men were riding on the same motorbike. They were coming from a party where they had been drinking, and were riding on a newly improved country road that replaced a bumpy dirt and stone track with an even gravel-topped surface. The result of this bit of development was that they drove faster on it at night and went off the edge, just before reaching Santa María. One of them, Miguel Angel, was killed.

One of my English students, Mario, was riding a motorbike with his girlfriend behind him on the road to San Ignacio, when a car came up fast behind them, with a drunken driver, and hit them in the rear. She was killed, and he survived. Particularly distressing was the case of another girl and her boyfriend, who went to San Ignacio at night on an icy road, on a wholly unnecessary journey. They had one crash helmet between them, and he gave it to her. They skidded at a corner and he was killed. Then there was the tragic case of a honeymoon couple from one of our country hamlets: they were both killed on their motorbike just a couple of days after they got married, journeying on the main highway without crash helmets.

Motorbikes

The number of victims of motorbike accidents almost doubled between 2006 and 2007, and in the first half of 2008 it more than doubled again: the number of traffic deaths per day rose from two to five, and half of those were motorbike accidents (*Ultima Hora, 1 October 2008*). According to the Ministry of Public Health and Social Wellbeing, deaths from traffic accidents in Paraguay have reached the level of an epidemic.

(*First published 4 April 2009.*)

ларл   സාസා

Dani's leg has healed completely, and he is now in his final year of studies at the Santa María Institute. A few people are now beginning to wear crash helmets. But motorbikes are still so dangerous that Peace Corps volunteers are sent immediately back home to the USA if they are seen riding one.

51

Monolith

Santa María de Fe has got into the national press because we knocked down a monolith bearing the name of Stroessner. It was a small, undistinguished marble block near the centre of the square, saying that electricity came to Santa María thanks to Alfredo Stroessner. He was the cruel dictator who sustained his regime of favouritism during 34 years (1954–89) by an extensive network of paid spies and torturers.

The Minister of the Interior at the time, and hence head of the torture operation, was Sabino Montanaro, who went into exile at the same time as Stroessner. Stroessner died in 2006 in Brazil, but Montanaro – who had sought sanctuary in Honduras – wanted to set foot again in his native land before his death. Perhaps the term is not apt, as he arrived in a wheelchair. He came unexpectedly during the night of 1 May, and was immediately admitted to the Police Hospital for studies.

His return unleashed a flood of pent-up anger from the victims and the bereaved relatives of those who had died under torture. Paraguay has at least 400 'disappeared' people, whose cases have never been clarified. The central point of the demonstrations against him was that he should say what had happened to the disappeared, and reveal where the bodies went.

It is a little thing to ask. But Montanaro has remained silent. The frail figure in the wheelchair, peeping nervously out above his swine-flu mask (he arrived in the middle of the hysteria about swine flu) is a far cry from the stout, arrogant man that used to smirk at Stroessner's side. All the same, the public outcry resulted in him being moved from the Police Hospital and locked up in the Tacumbú prison. His family managed to get him out of there a couple of days later, but it gave some satisfaction to the victims that at least he had spent two nights in prison for his crimes of imprisoning and torturing so many innocent people.

Here in Paraguay there has been no process of repentance for the past, no community rejection of the horrors of the repression. The Stroessner regime sowed terror in the hearts, and when Stroessner was replaced by a relative from the same Colorado political party, the fear eased but was never definitively lifted.

Even today, few people have any idea of what went on. Every year, when I receive a new intake of students in my Bible classes at the Santa María Institute, I ask them if they have heard of the *Ligas Agrarias Cristianas*. No one ever has. And yet this was the *campesino* Christian association that first flourished here in Misiones before going nation-wide, teaching that we are all brothers and sisters of equal dignity. It was bloodily wiped out by Stroessner's police as a subversive organisation, and wiped out of the memory too.

We are beginning to recover the memory now, bit by bit, through the wall hangings made by our craft workshop, and through the *Casa de las Victimas* museum in the neighbouring town of San Ignacio. Last year the *Verdad y Justicia* (Truth and Justice) commission completed their report, gathering together thousands of witness statements. But people do not talk much about the repression. The former spies and their families and the former victims and their families live side by side in a place like Santa María, and get on by not talking about the past.

Needless to say, President Fernando Lugo is a supporter of those who want to recover the memory. And – in the uprise of emotion stirred by Montanaro's return – he signed a resolution approving a change of name of the Colegio Nacional Santa Rosa (in our neighbouring town) to the Colegio Nacional Silvano Ortellado Flores, in honour of a *campesino* whose throat was cut in front of his wife and children, and who was then hanged from a tree in what is now the school garden. This was done by the local police force in 1976, because he had been a member of the *Ligas Agrarias Cristianas*.

Unfortunately, those who had this excellent idea had not reckoned on the school headmistress, whose husband had been a member of the congress in Stroessner's government. She mobilised the pupils in a demonstration through the streets to reject the change of name. This messy conflict has not yet been resolved.

In Santa María, when one of the former victims, Saturnino Uliambre, took an axe to the monument bearing the name of Stroessner, it might be thought that this was as a laudatory upsurge of popular feeling. In fact, much popular feeling went against it. The Colorado mayor and even the parish priest were furious at what they declared was an act of vandalism; many others took the same view, and the police are considering what punitive measures to take against the instigators of the destruction. Perhaps what they need to hear are voices from other countries assuring them that in the eyes of the world the vandalism against human bodies in the Stroessner torture chambers fully deserves a symbolic public action, such as the destruction of a small block of stone.

(*First published 4 July 2009.*)

ᐅᐈᐈ   ᐈᐈᐅ

The headmistress of Santa Rosa was successful in her campaign, and as a small compromise there is a plan to open an institute of alternative education with the name of Silvano Ortellado Flores.

52

Spring fever

It must be the effect of the spring, just officially beginning in Paraguay. No, it's not just that, it's Paraguay itself, this wonderful country, that makes me so full of enthusiasm. In these months I have been writing flat out to get a guidebook delivered to the publishers in time. I write at night till I cannot stifle the yawns any longer, and then wake before dawn, bright and keen to leap up and carry on writing. The more I write, the more I love my adopted country.

I have a new volunteer just arrived, to help in our English-teaching programme, and that has given another boost to sharing the joys of Paraguay. He came round today, just as I was about to say goodbye to Marcos Lucena, one of the best harpists in the country and our teacher here, so I asked Marcos as a favour to get out his harp and play. And he did, with his top pupil Victoria Oviedo, now beginning to be a professional harpist herself. '*Tren lechero.*' Wow! And there, captured in the virtuoso notes of the harp, were all the steam and puff and clickety click and whistles of these old chuffa chuffas – that people everywhere are so nostalgic about, and that we have still working in Paraguay.

Then they played Mangoré's *Danza Paraguaya*, which must be the most addictive music ever written. Da, da, dum-de-de-da, etc. And then it begins all over again, over and over, and you want it to go on forever.

Mangoré was the most talented guitar composer of all time (or so said the English guitarist John Williams) and he grew up right here in Misiones, in San Juan, the capital of our *departamento*. He was baptised Agustín Pio Barrios, but he loved his country so much that he took as his professional name the name of a historic indigenous leader, and preceded it with his Christian name spelled backwards, so he became Nitsuga Mangoré.

Marcos' taxi came, but he kept it waiting, as he and Victoria were absorbed in their art, playing on and on. Zipoli's *Allegro* came next, and the spirits of the past came alive again, the spirits of the Guaraní that built Santa María de Fe, with its adobe houses surrounded by long colonnades. (We have one still standing, and two replicas around the square, of which one is my house.)

The 'lost paradise' of the Jesuit-Guaraní reductions has inspired some 1,500 books and academic articles, but less well known are the Franciscan reductions, though they have left us with more church remains than the Jesuit towns. The beautiful carvings of the reredos in the Franciscan church of Caazapá left me speechless with wonder. I never knew it was there, and could not understand why no one had ever told me that there was a work of such simple and subtle loveliness in that far-off town.

There are so many joys of Paraguay, like the *mburucuyá* fruits (passion fruits, you say in English) with their hard yellow skins and orangey jellied pips inside, and their tangy flavour, which transforms any fruit salad. The *mburucuyá* flower is the Paraguayan national flower, and its rose-like petals are carved in stone and wood all around the reductions. The avocados are just coming into season now: a friend came round with a big bag of them, and no, he did not want any money. Abundance is the rule in the *campo* – nature gives in basketfuls and cartloads. And the cart, of course, is horse-drawn; it comes to my house once a week with vegetables.

Bird-watchers have a field day here: the *estancia* of Laguna Blanca, with its mixed landscape known as Cerrado, is said by the birders to be 'one of the best preserved reserves you can find in the south of South America'. You can relax on the white sands of the crystalline lagoon, or go on horseback through the woods, and be enthused by the number of species of birds you will find. And I have been writing about the 'effortless bi-lingualism' of Paraguay. How we English struggle to learn a language, as though to speak two languages were a feat beyond the normal! And here the simplest *campesino* can do it without thinking.

Then I have been writing about the folk dance, with the men snapping their horsewhips and stamping their boots, and the girls in their swirling *ñandutí* dresses, with their swinging plaits and flowers in their hair, charming and enticing the men, and certainly in the end having the upper hand of the romance. And the intricacy of the best *ao po'i* cloth, such that a large tablecloth, if made by one person single-handed, would take her a year and a half. And people are still making such things!

'A lost paradise?' People should rather say 'a paradise waiting to be discovered'.

(*First published 26 September 2009.*)

53

The Trinity of Trinidad

There are moments in life when we feel we are in the presence of something so historic and beautiful and unexpected, that we are lost for words and do not want to move on. I have had a few such moments in the research I have been doing for *The Bradt Guide to Paraguay*. One was in my most recent visit to the famous reduction of Trinidad, where there are ruins of a magnificent old Jesuit church and of the houses in the mission. I had been there many times before, usually with groups and usually under some time pressure, but this time I went alone.

I was determined to see the carving of the Trinity that I knew existed, from photographs. I had often asked after it, but it is kept in the modern church, adjoining the precinct of the ruins, accessible only from the other side of the fence, and to gain access, the guides have to collect the key from someone in the village. So this time I booked my visit in advance.

When I stepped inside the door of the undistinguished modern church, I almost wanted to fall to my knees before the carving, it was so mystical. The Trinity takes the form of God the Father stretching out his arms in parallel to those of his crucified Son, with a large Holy Spirit dove also stretching out its wings on the top of the cross. Even the rays of the Father's halo and the loose ends of the Son's loincloth echo the parallel lines of self-giving.

There is damage to the hands and noses and the beak of the bird that I had not noticed in the photograph, but that did not seem to matter. With the intricately painted wounds of Christ, the solemn, silent expression on the Father's face, and the expansive stretch of the dove's wings, the piece emits a spirit of sadness, peace and majesty, all at the same time.

What I love so much about these Paraguayan Trinities – for this is the most famous of many similar portrayals – is the importance they give to the Holy Spirit, which is carved larger than the tiny dove customarily shown in West-European Trinity paintings, of the sort that has been called dismissively 'Hunt the Pigeon'. Not only that, but there is a theological profundity in the dove being released out of the death of Christ on the cross.

This is deeply biblical, for the Greek of all four gospels, in slightly different phrases, expresses the idea of the release of the Spirit, in the very words used for dying. We clumsily capture it in English with phrases like 'he breathed his last' or 'he gave up the ghost', but a better translation would be 'he breathed out his Spirit'.

Even today, the Paraguayan saint-makers, or *santeros*, working in the villages of Tobatí and Capiatá, carve the Trinity in this traditional Paraguayan form. It is truly a three-in-one, as the persons of the Trinity are quite distinct, but are bound together in an inter-relationship of common movement towards humanity.

The preciousness of this particular piece is highlighted by the fact that it was stolen in 2006, and recovered in rather miraculous fashion. Three thieves had forced entry by night and taken it – not from this church, but from one next door that is falling into some disrepair. Reading about the theft, I was sad that I had never even set eyes on the work, but only knew it from a photograph.

But bizarrely, one of the thieves died shortly afterwards in a traffic accident, and shortly afterwards a second one of the trio also died. The third thief was then so frightened that the justice of God would get him as well, that he confessed to his crime and led the police to where the figure was buried, by the bank of the Río Paraná, where it was waiting to be smuggled across the river into Argentina.

But my amazement was not restricted solely to this figure. What was a complete surprise was the quantity and the quality of the other statues in the church, all of Jesuit-Guaraní origin. Crowded one on top of each other, in much too small a space and with no attempt at presentation, were the most amazing Virgins and Trinities, crucifixes and risen Christs, angels and pedestals – all in all, statues of equal beauty to the best in the great museums of Santa María or San Ignacio.

I had the excitement of an explorer, discovering what is known only by the local people, who do not fully realise its significance. When one day these pieces receive a worthy setting, Trinidad will be seen for what it is – the reduction *par excellence* for both ruins and statues.

(*First published 2 January 2010.*)

54

Laura

February is always an exciting time, because it is when I finalise which new students will receive scholarships from the Santa María Education Fund, before the academic year begins. There is a particular thrill in discovering new people of intelligence, many of whom I have never met before. One of these is Laura – a delightful little person with a lot of bounce. She looks less than her 18 years, but when she tells her story you sense a depth of maturity. In fact she is getting married in a week's time.

Laura comes from a *compañía* called San Antonio, which is one of the furthest outposts in the municipality. Her life has been shaped by her love for her father, who is no longer alive but who still exercises a deep influence on her. He used to work as a farm labourer, until he had a terrible accident, when she was still a young child. He had climbed up on the back of a tractor to clean the blades of the machine that ploughed the earth. His workmate either did not hear or did not understand what he had said he was doing, for he turned the engine on, making the blades whirr round and cut deep into the other's body. Laura's father was left with missing bits of flesh, covered over with loose skin. He could never work again.

When Laura was in primary school her father spoke to her solemnly about her less-than-perfect marks. 'I will never now be able to pay for further education for you,' he said. 'To stand any chance of getting a scholarship you will have to study really hard and get nothing less than the top mark in every subject, every year. Alternatively you can relax now, but know that there will be no further education for you later on. The choice is yours.' Laura thought about it overnight and went back to her father: 'I have decided to go all out for the top marks,' she said.

The next year her father was taken ill, after he had gone out in the blazing sun against doctor's orders to attend to an emergency in his field. As he was taken by ambulance to hospital in Asunción he asked for Laura's forgiveness. 'Why?' she asked. 'Because now the little money I had saved up to buy you a moped, so you could go to secondary school in Santa María, will be spent on my ambulance and my treatment.' 'Never mind,' said Laura, 'it is better for me to miss a year of secondary school than for you to be unable to go to hospital.' He never returned home.

Six years later when she left school, Laura did indeed get the top marks. She wants to study social work, so she can help other people in need, and she is in a good position to get a state scholarship. But even when this is confirmed it will only cover her fees, with nothing left over to cover her fares or study materials. The Santa María Education Fund will pay the balance, and advance the university costs until the state scholarship comes through.

Laura was one of the clear-cut cases for help, but to help allocate resources justly among other applicants with good marks, from deep in the *campo*, we held an exam. The exams are on my desk now, and I am enthused as I read them. The essay question was suggested to me by a visitor to the Santa María Hotel, who likes to ask young people what they are most proud of in their country.

'In my country people are simple and kind,' wrote one, 'and they receive a stranger as a family member, with open arms and without any kind of discrimination. Another of the great values the Paraguayan has is the typical Guaraní greeting "*Mba'éichapa*?" ("How are you?") to which you always reply "Very well", even when things are bad.'

'Paraguay is the only bilingual country where two languages are spoken,' said another. 'We speak Spanish and our beloved Guaraní, in honour of our ancestors who defended our country with their lives.'

Another answer was, 'Paraguayan dance and the polka make you happy and fill you with joy, at the patronal feastdays held in the countryside.' And another, 'My country still has much of what God has left us: trees which give fruit and shade, where we can hear the song of the birds and the insects; beautiful fields where the animals find pasture; a lot of land to cultivate, hills and streams to enjoy, and pure air to breathe.'

I hope that Paraguay will have reason to be proud of these young people in due course, who are now so proud of their country.

(*First published 27 February 2010.*)

55

Madame Lynch

When I came to Paraguay I had never heard of Madame Lynch. Now I have lived here for ten years, it is inconceivable not to have heard of her. It would be like not having heard of Winston Churchill. As an English-woman I was particularly expected to have heard of her, because she lived part of her life in England, and claimed on at least two occasions to be English – although actually she was born in Ireland. The 'Madame' comes from the fact that she was married to a Frenchman before she moved to Paraguay.

I am not the only person who came to Paraguay without having heard of Madame Lynch. Another was Irish writer Michael Lillis, who then became so fascinated by her that he wrote a book, *The Lives of Eliza Lynch: scandal and courage* (Michael Lillis and Ronan Fanning, Gill and Macmillan 2009). On his first visit to Asunción in the early 1990s he was asked by the then President, 'What do they say in Ireland about our national heroine?' Lillis recounts:

'I had no idea what he was talking about, but I did my best (I had been, for what it's worth, a diplomat in my country's service for 20 years). "It is a subject of intense interest, Excellency", "I replied. As soon as we left the Palace, I said to Esteban: "Who *is* the national heroine of this country?"'

That weekend Lillis returned to Ireland, and sought out academic colleagues. 'Have any of you heard of this woman?' he asked them.

Nobody had. Three days later, an erudite professor at University College Dublin sent him a slim volume – *The World's Wickedest Women* (Margaret Nicholas, London 1984) – that included her story. Lillis attempts to refute that reputation. But he does not do it the Paraguayan way – by letting her bask in the reflected glory of the alleged heroism of her lover, the nineteenth-century President Francisco Solano López. On the contrary, he does it by blaming Mariscal López for the crimes laid on Eliza's shoulders: he alleges that she had no option but to be loyal to him because otherwise she would have been tortured by her lover as a traitor, along with all his other victims.

I first came across her name when I visited the (now defunct) wax-work museum in Asunción, and was told that this glamour-girl was the mistress of Mariscal López. Then I kept on hearing her name in the news because it was also the name of the ring road, the completion of which seemed to be endlessly delayed. Gradually I came to realise how much the Paraguayans adored her – because she had style and charm and extravagant jewellery; because she was hated by the other rich society ladies of her era and so became a figurehead for the poor; and most of all because she loved and was loyal to the end to Mariscal López, who is bizarrely regarded as the country's greatest hero.

Mariscal López, supported by Madame Lynch, led his country into the Triple Alliance War – a war so catastrophic that it resulted in the death of an estimated 99% of the adult males, and somewhere between 58% and 75% of the entire population. Was Eliza – as the next rulers of Paraguay declared – 'a monument of infamy and public scandal' who 'at the side of the tyrant performed the most criminal and impure relations'? Or was she rather as the contemporary Argentinian journalist Hector Varela described her? 'Her eyes were of an azure that seemed borrowed from the primary colour of the sky; they held an expression of ineffable sweetness and emitted waves of light where Cupid floated and sipped of happiness and love ...' Etc.

Just as fascinating is the interpretation of the Triple Alliance War. Every Sunday my newspaperman brings me a new instalment in comic form of the history of this utterly appalling war, told for children, with all the drama designed to elicit from them feelings of national pride and self-sacrifice – just the kind of interpretation that was convenient in

Stroessner's 34-year dictatorship, to encourage the populace to be long-suffering. Here is a snippet from the battle of Piribebúy:

A group of wounded soldiers sit around a fire in a freezing August night. The commander says: 'We have 1,600 soldiers for the defence of the town, of whom only 200 are really prepared for fighting. The rest are women, children and old people.' An elder councillor says, '1,600 against some 20,000 allies? We can no longer fight for the country, we can only die for it.' The commander asks, 'And are you afraid to die, Captain Solalinde?' He replies, 'No, it isn't that.' The commander says, 'Whoever wishes is free to leave. But if you decide to stay and fight with me, we will show the enemy that although they bring chains to enslave us or canons to kill us, the spirit of the Paraguayan is and will always be free. It does not matter what obstacles destiny places in our path. What matters is the decisions we take. And if we die for our principles, I promise you that our deaths will find an echo in the history of our country.' A wounded soldier, with a bandage on his head and one eye missing, throws open his arms and cries out with enthusiasm, 'I propose a cheer for our commander. Hip hip hurrah!' And the echo of hurrahs fills the night air. Etc.

I am unsure whether to deplore or admire this glorification of carnage, but I do find riveting the skill of the artist, with his atmospheric nights around camp fires, rearing horses, blood-spattered bandages, swords glinting in the sun, pealing church bells, and fierce-faced semi-naked half-starved boy-soldiers yelling at the top of their young voices 'Victory or death!!!' It all makes for the kind of larger-than-life drama in which a woman like Madame Lynch inevitably gains immortality.

(*First published 29 May 2010.*)

56

Drunken driving

This is not the first time I have written about a motorbike accident and I am terribly afraid it will not be the last. I had been looking forward to my Sunday – supposedly my one day off, though for months on end I had had no day off. I had even selected the novel I was going to read – *La Babosa* by Paraguayan writer Gabriel Casaccia – and it was sitting there still in its cellophane cover waiting to be opened, as I made my coffee. Then the phone rang: not my normal phone, which has an answer machine, as I had unplugged it during a storm the previous night, but my secondary phone in my bedroom, with its tinkling little ring. 'Have you heard about the accident?'

There are so many motorbike accidents that you might wonder why I should be writing about yet another one. But this one came closer to home than any other and also showed up vividly the ghastly injustice of the Paraguayan justice system. One of the two lads on the motorbike was Diego, brother of Adrián, the boyfriend of one of our former English volunteers, Chloe. The other was Picuno, the only son of Julia of the organic sugar cooperative. Both were friends of my own son. Both were killed.

Diego was coming home for the weekend, having just earned his month's wages in Asunción. He reached San Ignacio (our nearest town, on the Ruta Uno highway) around 8.30 pm, when it was dark and beginning to rain. He rang a friend of mine who has a motorbike and asked if she would go to collect him. She does not do that journey after nightfall even when it is not raining, so she was afraid to go. My first reaction when I heard this was 'Thank God she did not go'. My second reaction was 'Oh my God, because she did not go, two people died'. She was broken with grief when she heard how things had worked out.

It was a couple more hours before Diego could find someone to go and collect him, and in those couple of hours the storm had hit full on, with thunder and lightning and torrential rain, before beginning to ease off. Picuno, who is a motorbike mechanic, went out on a friend's bike, and joked as Diego mounted on, 'You had better behave yourself, or we won't get home safely.' Neither were wearing helmets, but no helmet would have saved them from the onslaught that was facing them.

Meanwhile, Franci Vargas from San Ignacio had taken two friends (one a law student and the other a junior official in the *Fiscalia* – the state prosecutor's office) to spend the day in Santa María and its surrounds. They went to a fiesta in San Fernando and drank. Then they went to a birthday party in Santa María and drank more. According to the class-mates of the law student in the group, when they left Santa María in their jeep they were driving very fast and there was very little visibility. Then there was an almighty crash, and the jeep slithered to a halt with the airbags ballooning out and black smoke coming out of the engine. 'Have we hit a cow?' they wondered. They got out of the jeep and walked back, to find a dead man and a motorbike in smithereens. The second body had been thrown further into the undergrowth, and was discovered later with one leg almost severed.

One of the first to pass was a witness called Raúl Orihuela, who stopped and was greeted abusively by the driver, Franci Vargas, who was standing there with a beer can in his hand. '*Entra en tu culo,*' he said, which means 'F___ off'. There were no breathalyser tests, due to shortage of resources, and the blood test was taken more than five hours after the accident. It took more than three weeks for the result to come through, but when it did it confirmed that Vargas was over the limit, despite the five-hour delay.

When I visited Picuno's house on the Sunday morning, I found Julia looking like Our Lady of Sorrows: dark, distraught and strangely beautiful, at the side of the open coffin where her son's body lay with one side of his face smashed in. 'Half an hour before the accident I was with him,' she wept. Diego's body had had one leg almost severed. The funeral is always done within 24 hours, but the dark falls early now in Paraguay, and during the day I was in constant communication by mobile-phone text with Chloe and Adrián, who had to take a bus from Concepción in the north of the country and then took a taxi for the last 250km. The funeral procession left Diego's house and made its slow way up to the junction with the main road, where Adrián and Chloe's taxi screeched to a halt one metre ahead of it.

The next afternoon I visited the site of the accident with Chloe and Adrián and took photos. The huge black stain and position of thousands of motorbike fragments showed beyond any doubt that the jeep was on the wrong side of the road.

And what about justice? If a driver is drunk and kills someone he can be guilty of *homicidio doloso* and in theory can go to prison for 15 years. But this case was classified by the *Fiscalía* from the start as *homicidio culposo* and has a lower penalty of 5 years' imprisonment or a fine. In practice no one ever goes to prison for this, because they prefer to pay the fine, and hardly anyone even goes to trial for it, because the law permits the victims' families to make a prior *arreglo amistoso* (or 'friendly settlement') with the author of the crime. The families get more money that way than by sharing out their portion of the fine with what is due to the courts and the lawyers, after the criminal has almost inevitably bribed the judge to give the most lenient sentence possible. Law students at university report that lesson one, day one, of their degree course teaches them that in Paraguay only the poor go to prison.

The families of Diego and Picuno are two of the poorest in Santa María, and they have been offered £1,400 each, as a 'friendly settlement'. I want to tell them – and I do tell them – not to accept it but to see the case through, no matter how long it takes. But then, I am not the person who is going to lose out.

(*First published 3 July 2010.*)

༒༒　　 ༒༒

An English volunteer who was here at the time organised a fund to pay for legal costs (www.justiceinparaguay.com), *and helped to arrange for a top-class lawyer to fight the case. With his powerful advocacy a settlement was made during the trial for the families to receive five times what Vargas had originally offered. The lawyer advised not pushing the criminal case further as he sensed that both fiscal and judge might have been bought off by Vargas. Vargas then defaulted on the amount he had agreed to pay, and it took months of pressure to get him to pay up what he had agreed.*

57

An Amnesty godmother

'The worst rapist was treated better than the political prisoner,' said Antonio González Arce, speaking from his personal experience of nearly 30 years ago in a Paraguayan jail. Today he lives on the outskirts of Asunción, and scrapes a living making leather Bible covers and keyrings. I came to know him through an Australian woman, Monica, who formed an extraordinary friendship with him in the early 1980s when he was Amnesty International's prisoner of the month. It made me realise how life-transforming the work of Amnesty can be.

The friendship Monica formed with Antonio is all the more remarkable for the fact that she never visited Paraguay and does not speak Spanish. She used a translator for her letters, carefully copying out the Spanish version. The repressive dictatorship of General Alfredo Stroessner ended in 1989, but years afterwards she wanted to get in touch with Antonio again, and wrote to me as a resident of Paraguay, care of *The Tablet*. She had lost contact, she explained, writing to the old addresses to no avail. 'I was only concerned that he should know that I have not forgotten him over the years.'

Finding an ex-political prisoner in Paraguay is not too difficult. I bumped into Antonio at a meeting to commemorate the anniversary of the *Pascua Dolorosa* – the series of arrests in Holy Week 1976 when the

Ligas Agrarias Cristianas were wiped out. Several of our local Christian leaders in Santa María de Fe and San Ignacio were taken away for years of torture. Antonio, who knew them all in prison, was one of many speakers at the commemorative event. When I told him I had been contacted by Monica he practically fell off his chair. 'She's my beloved godmother,' he said, 'an enormously important spiritual presence in my life.'

I promised to visit him in Asunción to give a fuller report to Monica, but for a long time my work commitments prevented me from fulfilling my promise. Finally, last week, I rang Antonio's number, and was put through to him. Again, Antonio responded in an amazing way to Monica's name. 'I was thinking of her just this morning,' he said, 'but I have not been at all well, and I was so afraid that I would die without being able to contact her again. I also had a presentiment that something had happened to her. Is she all right? Is she still alive? She has not been answering my letters.' I told him that she had the same experience, that her letters were not getting through. But I had to admit I had had no news of her for a long time, and promised to find out.

I sent an email to Monica but it bounced. An internet search threw up a phone number that might or might not be hers. I tried it early one morning, and got straight through to her: it was 11 o'clock at night in Australia but she had not yet turned off her light. She emailed me the next day: 'I was so excited at your phone call that I could not sleep for some time.'

Antonio had fallen under suspicion in the Stroessner regime because he used to visit the family of a political prisoner who was a Communist. He himself had been in the Party for a short time but had left it several years before he was imprisoned. He did not help his case by telling the judge that he considered himself a revolutionary. He spent seven years in prison, including several months of being locked up in a cupboard, all through the sweltering weather of December and January.

He had regular correspondence with two Australian members of Amnesty. One of them, Jan, was all activity and energy, he said, while Monica, by contrast, was all tenderness and heart. During the years he spent in prison (1982–6 and 1986–7) Antonio was seen as a tower of strength by his fellow inmates, but when he was finally released the pent-up tension broke out in him and he felt himself near to going mad. He could not take a bus without having an irrational conviction that it was on the point of a crash. Fortunately his beautiful ballerina wife, Flora, stood by him, though Antonio told her he would not be angry if she found it all too much and left him.

After my visit, I sent photos to Monica, and she wrote successfully this time to Antonio. He replied to her: 'Thanks to you I had the strength to overcome all the discouragement and depression that I had. Even after all I had suffered, I went on working in social movements after my release, and with Amnesty. I showed them the letters that you sent, and everyone was moved, even to tears.'

(*First published 4 September 2010.*)

58

The storm

People talk of the quiet after the storm, but they do not usually mean as much quiet as we had after Wednesday night's storm. On Friday morning – two days later – my electricity was still off. In the more rural areas of Santa María, it was off for five days.

We had a very hot day, and there had been plenty of warning of the storm. The newspaper had forecast it, and there was about an hour of lightning flashes on the horizon, shortly after dusk, before any rain fell. I brought inside everything from the garden of my house except for a very old table and two large plastic bowls, which, being full of water, I thought would be safe from blowing away. I was wrong.

Safe inside with all windows and doors tight shut, I heard the sharp pinging of hailstones pounding the glass. The wind must have been driving the hail almost horizontal, as water was finding its way in between the shut window and its frame – not in dribbles but in streams that ran into fast-expanding eddies on the floor, soaking through entire newspapers that I threw in their path. The rain was even coming in through my heavy panelled outside door – not just under it and around it but through the middle of it, forcing its way through the joints of panels and frame and running down the wood. Meanwhile on the opposite side of the house, sheltered from the wind, no rain came in, but you could see the lightning flashes making a continuous palpitating light display.

But this was nothing compared to what some of my students were to suffer in their more precarious homes: some lost roofs, one had an outside wall fall down as well. When I next saw a newspaper, I saw how the hail had peppered roofs with holes.

It is normal in Paraguay for electricity to cut out during a storm, and we supply ourselves with candles and torches to see us through. Once the next day's dawn comes, the power supply is usually swiftly repaired. But when there is no knowing how many days you will be cut off for, life takes on a whole new aspect.

The first service to go after electricity is the water supply, as power is needed to work the pumps. I had eight litres of emergency water, but by the end of Thursday I was down to my last bottle. Every time I opened my fridge door I was letting in warm air, so on Thursday evening I decided to cook all my meat before it went off. Fortunately we cook by calor gas, so that was one service that was unaffected. But I was left with greasy roasting pans that I could not wash up.

The streets were silent: no radios, no music, not even cars and motorbikes because the people cannot afford to fill up their tanks but survive on a little petrol that they put in for each journey, and now the petrol pumps were not working. It is a long tradition that children and teachers do not go to school when it has been raining, because they get muddy on the way, so no one was out on the streets. The town was as quiet as the grave.

Most forms of work were impossible. I can go on working on my computer by battery power for an hour or two, but I did not dare run down the battery completely without any idea of when I would be able to recharge it. Of course my printer did not work, and needless to say there was no internet. The mobile phones lost their signals, and very soon ran out of battery as well. My volunteer Sarah came round to see me in the early evening of Thursday announcing that she no longer had any way of knowing what the time was, since she normally depended on her mobile phone for this information.

There was no television of course, but Sarah brought the news that someone with a battery radio had heard that it was not just Santa María that was without power but all of Misiones, and that half a dozen huge pylons had fallen. We could be days without power. It was not until the next day's newspaper arrived that I discovered that 35 per cent of Paraguay had been cut off.

I could not clean my house because I had no water. The table outside the back door was torn to shreds and lying in the mud: when I picked up the pieces I got mud on my hands that I could not wash off for lack of water. One plastic bowl had completely disappeared, even though I walked for a long way looking for it. The other had been recovered by a neighbour from the far side of her garden, but it now had a hole in its side and was useless.

One of the few things I could do was practice my harp. I could also tidy my house and reorder my files – and this was a very welcome opportunity, though I ran out of tidying to do. When the night came again I read my novel by candlelight. When I finished it I went to bed.

Going to bed early meant I woke early the next morning, when it was still dark. I switched on my light and nothing happened. I tried to get back to sleep and failed, so I got up and opened the shutters. Then I could not think of anything more to do so I went back to bed.

I began to think, 'What if the electricity is off for a long time?' I would have to go to Asunción to find somewhere where my computer would work. But how would I get there if I could not put petrol in my engine? And how would the buses work if they could not fill up either? Even if some buses kept going, how would I get money out for the journey if the cash machines were not working for lack of power?

For many centuries, electricity did not exist, and yet great civilisations were built. But the people travelled on horseback, and we have lost the riding skills. Money was passed from hand to hand, travelling from one continent to another by ship over many months, not drawn instantaneously out of an English bank account via a cash machine. But in today's globalised world, a people without electricity is a people without work, without water, without food, without hygiene, without money; a people without communication, a people without a voice.

And then, suddenly, the lights came on, and my apocalyptic thoughts came to an end.

(*First published 30 October 2010.*)

59

World Cup

At last the world has sat up and paid attention to Paraguay – in the World Cup. We always knew we were good, but it is gratifying when other people begin to notice it too. In the end we went down by just one goal to the team that were to become the champions – again by just one goal. We did as well against the champions as the runners-up did.

Men, women and children wore the shirt of the *albirrojas* (red and whites) every day there was a World Cup match: at the supermarket checkouts, at the petrol pumps, in hotel receptions, and everywhere. All looked very elegant in them, particularly young women whose curves were enhanced by the vertical stripes. Here in Paraguay there is no fuss about copyright: you pay a lot more for an authentic football shirt, and the average Paraguayan cannot afford it. But piracy is the rule and cheaper versions abound within the economic reach of the majority.

This was not the first time Paraguay had qualified for a World Cup. We have qualified for the last four, which is an amazing feat for a country with such a small population, lack of infrastructure, and general level of poverty. But this year Paraguay had possibly the best team ever. We qualified this time ahead of Argentina, who are always among the top favourites.

The match that knocked us out was an unbelievable sequence of cliff-hangers. I watched the 3 July match with my adopted 'family' here in

Santa María – three generations and a few friends arranged around the television set on the outside patio. Paraguay belted the ball into the net – and had the goal disallowed: we thought it was 1–0 but it wasn't. Then we were awarded a penalty against Spain. The sweat was running off the grave, nervous face of Oscar 'Tacuara' ('Bamboo') Cardozo as he stood waiting to shoot. We thought it was 1–0 again, but it wasn't, because the penalty was saved.

Then minutes later a penalty was awarded against Paraguay: how could we have allowed that to happen? Xabi Alonso knocked the ball neatly into the net and our spirits plummeted. We thought it was 0–1, but it wasn't, because the goal was disallowed for invasion into the penalty area. It was taken again – and the goal was saved! It was 0–0 after all! We leaped into the air and hugged each other. But the joy did not last till the end. Spain managed to get the ball into the net less than ten minutes before the end.

The front page of the *Ultima Hora* newspaper the next morning had a brilliant picture of a crowd in Asunción's main shopping street Palma – everyone dressed in the *albirroja* shirt – with dropping jaws, frozen expressions and hands held to the head in horror when Spain scored their goal. But afterwards we were philosophical about losing. We felt we had had a good run for our money. We could not escape, however, a sense of what might have been: what if someone else had taken our penalty?

The match a few days earlier against Japan was different. All the way through the 0–0 match and the 0–0 extra time we felt we were better, that we ought to win, that we had to win, that victory was always just eluding our grasp. When it came to penalties I could hardly bear to watch. But the joy, the joy, when we won! Out on the streets of Santa María a *caravana* began. A *caravana* is a slow-moving procession of cars, motorbikes and bicycles, all tooting their horns and flashing their lights to indicate a celebration. Most commonly people do *caravanas* for political reasons – to show the strength of the Colorado Party, or when Fernando Lugo won the presidential election. The joy of the *caravana* this time was that everyone was rejoicing – not one group against another, but the whole country united in jubilation, because Paraguay had reached the quarter-finals of the World Cup for the first time ever.

As it happened, I had to rush that day to the next town to get to the bank before it closed, and I found myself in San Ignacio in the midst of a *caravana* without intending it. Everyone was waving Paraguayan flags and many had the flag painted on their cheeks. The *caravana* passed, and went around the block, and passed again, and again, and again, while those working in the shops came to the doors to watch. I lost count of how many times it went around the central streets of San Ignacio. For a little country, an ignored country, a country that people are always getting muddled up with Uruguay or with Peru, to be suddenly the focus of world attention was amazing! History was made that day.

(*First published 31 July 2010.*)

Afterword

In one of my pieces ('My new house' p.127) I wrote about the wonderful new house I had built – a replica of the *casas de indios* that once stood around the square. It was a luxury for me, but for Santa María it was an attempt to restore something of the original beauty of the square.

But the update on my house is tragic. Almost as soon as I moved in it became evident that the house had problems, because the plaster was cracking and falling off the walls (see 'Mural' p.136). I paid Nino Sotelo, the artist of the mural, double the price that I had originally agreed with him, when I realised that he was going to lose his entire creation of six weeks' work. I felt I had become unwitting partner of a crime against art, and when I spoke to my friends about what had happened I could not hold back my tears.

But little did I realise then just how serious the problems were. Within two years it was discovered that the roof beams were not holding up the roof, but that gaps were appearing between wall and rafters and beams. The fundamental construction of the house was wrong, because the adobe blocks had been used like bricks, to support a roof. In fact, the adobe buildings of the Jesuit-Guaraní era supported the roof on strong wooden columns, and added adobe walls afterwards to fill in the space, as windbreaks. My roof was compressing the adobe, buckling the plaster,

184

pushing the walls out of true, and causing gaps to open up. I had in fact asked Pedro during the construction why he was building the walls before the roof, knowing that the Guaraní did it differently, and had never received a satisfactory answer.

Not only that, but a geotechnical study – not done before – declared that the ground was unusually soft and that much stronger foundations were needed. Inserting these extraordinarily strong foundations under a house that was already standing has been enormously expensive.

Then it was decided to take some sample adobe blocks for analysis of their weight-bearing properties. When they were removed from the wall they were so crumbly they had to be transported in bubble-wrap in an attempt to get them to Asunción before they fell apart. They were found to be so fragile that the test could not even be performed on them. No one quite knows why this is, but the current theory is that the heavy rains that fell after the walls were built, but before they were roofed over, had left the adobe so sodden that the chemical composition was permanently altered. The blocks had originally been dried out safely under cover.

Finally, the roof tiles, which had been made in Santa María in a supposedly exciting re-activation of an old tile-making factory, turned out to be so brittle that they all had to be replaced.

With new foundations, new walls and a new roof, what remained of the old house that could be re-used? Only the wood: the windows, the doors and the wooden columns.

The cost of building my house the first time had been 339 million guaraníes, which was £30,000 at the time. The cost of rebuilding it is also going to total 339 million guaraníes, which at today's exchange rate is now equivalent to £56,000. I cannot really afford to pay this money twice over, but I have had no choice but to rebuild: I could not go on living in the house because it was in danger of collapsing on me, and I would have left the village with a modern ruin on its beautiful old square. Pedro has no means of paying me the compensation that he owes me, and insurance for such matters is unheard of in Paraguay.

Bearing in mind that almost half the cost of the new house is in its new foundations, it now emerges that my original house could have cost less. It cost more than necessary because I wanted to employ local people and pay them a just daily wage rather than agree a fixed price in advance. One of the problems of this poor country is that the economy cannot support a just daily wage. The legally established minimum wage is only paid by the larger firms, because small outfits cannot possibly afford to pay an amount that gives people a decent standard of living.

I did in fact notice at the beginning that I was being expected to pay a number of labourers to stand around and do nothing, and I asked for the workforce to be reduced. The architects of the new house insisted on bringing in builders they knew from Asunción, so that they could give me in advance a contract with a price and a date they could guarantee, knowing that the builders would deliver good work and on time. My principles of giving all the work to the local poor flew out of the window.

The construction in adobe had been an exciting dream. The basic difference between brick and adobe is that brick is baked and adobe just dries in the sun. It has different qualities, both technically and aesthetically. Pedro wanted to show the people of Santa María that the ancient technique of adobe building worked, and that it was cheaper, so that people would then have the confidence to build adobe houses for themselves at lower cost. I knew that earth construction was now being rediscovered and redeveloped with great success in many countries of the world. But in Paraguay, now, the failure of my house is likely to set back by many years any future attempts to build in adobe. In any case, adobe construction is only cheaper if you make the mud blocks yourself. If you pay someone else by the day to make them for you, it works out more expensive.

As for the roof tiles, that had been another innovative project for the financial future of the village, begun with the best of intentions. The town of Tobatí is where roof tiles are generally made, but Pedro had originally told me (though later he changed his advice) that we could not buy from there tiles of sufficient size to fit in with the old Jesuit-Guaraní design. Reactivating Santa María's disused *olería*, or tile-making factory, therefore seemed to kill two birds with one stone: it would provide my house with the big tiles that were traditional on buildings of the Jesuit-Guaraní era, and it would re-activate a new and traditional industry in Santa María, so that there could be a new source of work for the future. What seems to have gone wrong was that the tiles were not baked for long enough, so they were not strong enough. But what also went wrong was that I was paying the workers per day, rather than per tile, with the result that each of these unusable tiles had cost me three times the cost of a good-quality tile from Tobatí.

I felt I had discovered a new meaning to the saying, 'The road to hell is paved with good intentions.'

But I cannot leave this book on such a gloomy note, so read on for a more cheerful event.

Final word

I have finished the editing of this book in the week that Paraguay celebrated the bicentenary of its Independence. It became independent from Spain on the night of 14–15 May 1811. It is not often that you get a chance to celebrate a centenary or one of its multiples: they come around not more than once in a lifetime. We are all over-stimulated to the point of happy exhaustion.

There are aspects of Paraguayan culture that even after 11 years here, I still have not properly taken in. And one of them is just how much the Independence means to the people. I have often heard them talk about it; I have celebrated the national holiday every year with them; I have visited the *Casa de la Independencia* where the plot was hatched; I have become familiar with the names of the *Próceres* – the individuals who carried out the plot so successfully that not a drop of blood was spilled; I have even written a chapter in a book published this year by a Paraguayan to celebrate the Independence ('The Jesuits' influence in National Identity' in *Paraguay 200*, ed. Robert Munro). Yet nothing had quite prepared me for the explosion of popular feeling that has broken out all over the country.

A whole month of activities began triumphantly with a fantastic concert at the former reduction of Jesús, bringing together the country's

188

top musicians to play all the patriotic music that could be thought of. Everyone in the audience had a flag to wave, or a long tri-coloured balloon. The backdrop of the ruins was bathed in red, white and blue light, and the evening ended with a firework display over the top of them.

During the next week, in Santa María, the children started practising their march for the Independence parade, bunting came out across the streets, and house after house was decorated with elaborately stretched, pleated or gathered flags of red, white and blue. Flags and bunting, parades and patriotic songs – all are familiar. But in the end nothing can compete with sheer spontaneous ecstasy. The municipality declared we would have no less than six days of holiday in a row.

In Asunción the Teatro Municipal of Asunción put on a free dramatisation of the history of the Independence and was full to bursting, with the aisles crammed full of people standing. The people sang, and clapped, and shouted, and waved, so that the division between actors and audience practically disappeared. The Minister of Culture, Ticio Escobar, a very distinguished elderly gentleman, went onto the stage in his suit and danced and sang along with the actors in period costume the Paraguayan equivalent of the English 'Land of Hope and Glory': *Patria Querida, somos tu esperanza, Somos la flor del bello porvenir.* 'Beloved country, we are your hope, We are the flower of your beautiful future.'

Over the weekend of 14 and 15 May everyone in Santa María watched the Asunción celebrations on television, but I went up to experience the events live. The tallest buildings in the capital were wrapped up like birthday presents with enormous swathes of red, white and blue cloth, draping from roof to ground. Huge pillars were swaddled with bands of material in the three colours. The *Panteón de los Héroes* was repainted (finished only just in time for 14 May) and had new floodlighting in subtly alternating sweeps of pink and blue light: simply beautiful.

Over the weekend of festivities there were displays of parachuting and ballooning, military displays, naval displays, airforce displays, a carnival parade, church bells pealing all over the country, concerts concerts concerts, and fireworks fireworks fireworks. The two most famous national buildings had brilliantly artistic multimedia displays projected onto their facades. And the crowds! Never in my life have I seen so many people – the vast riverside area crammed with people as far as the eye could see.

Two days later Santa María held its own parade – bigger than we have ever had before. This time I and my English volunteers took part alongside three of our Paraguayan students who are also now English teachers. We walked behind the Institute students, who were beautifully dressed in traditional costume, the girls in long gathered dresses and the men barefoot and with machetes, with the traditional *faja* or cummerbund around their waist; there was even an ox cart to complete the Institute's display. 'You are properly Paraguayan now,' said one of my friends, 'wearing the flag, going in the parade, singing *Patria Querida*.'

No one knows how to celebrate the way Latin Americans do: their *alegría* is legendary. I have talked of and taught liberation theology for years, but never fully taken on board that liberation means not only from sin and from poverty but also the liberation of the nation – liberation from the colonial power of Spain on the one hand, and from the neighbouring power of Argentina on the other. (Argentina fought battles earlier in the same year of 1811 in a bid to include Paraguay in its own newly independent nation.)

Here in Santa María the children asked one of our volunteer English teachers when our own country celebrated its Independence. All the countries they had ever heard of celebrated their Independence, so Britain must surely have done so too. Sheepishly he admitted that we were the colonisers, the ones that others had to seek their independence from. 'We don't come too well out of this,' he admitted.

Much of this book has been about poverty and pain, in the struggle of a third-world country to move forward. But much of it has also been about their joy and festivities. It is appropriate now that *alegría* should have the final word.

¡Viva el Paraguay!

Santa María Craft

www.santamariadefe.com
info@santamariadefe.com

The *Taller de Hermandad* cooperative began in 1989 and now comprises 35 women from poor homes. They specialize in appliqué embroidery, and make bags, hangings and clothes, with designs from everyday life in the countryside.

An intimate hotel on the historic square with a library and a thatched chapel

Santa María Hotel

www.santamariahotel.org ✆ info@santamariahotel.org
Santa María de Fe, Misiones, Paraguay. 00 595 981 861553

Santa Maria Education Fund

The Santa Maria Education Fund gives scholarships to bright students from poor homes in Paraguay, with an emphasis on tertiary education. It pays for university courses, English exams, music lessons, human rights education and many other classes, and runs an Institute with a free two-year course in food technology. Please support us if you can.

Accountancy, Agriculture, Bible, Biochemistry, Business administration, Dentistry, English, Food technology, French, Harp, IT, Italian, Latin, Law, Mechanics, Medicine, Musical theory, Nursing, Nutrition, Pedagogy, Social Work, Tourism, Violin

info@santamariadefe.org   www.santamariadefe.org   UK reg.charity 1105031

Bradt's Paraguay is the first dedicated travel guide to the country

Having lived in Paraguay since 2000 the author Margaret Hebblethwaite has intimate knowledge of the country

Bradt
travel guides

"Words fail me in attempting to praise adequately your masterly Bradt Guide to Paraguay"
(Adrian J. English, author of *Paraguayan Revolutions of the XX Century*)

www.bradtguides.com